It's a Marathon, Not a Sprint

My Road to the Marathon and Ph.D.

Vanessa R. Corcoran

To our greatest joy, Lucy. Thank you for being the brightest light, especially in times of darkness.

Foreword

The common phrase "it's a marathon, not a sprint" is meant to help us slow down when we are trying to achieve our goals. It aims to remind us to take things one step at a time, and to respect the process of attaining a goal. In a world where everything seems to be moving faster and faster all the time, we often need this reminder to help keep us steady and grounded. For Vanessa, this concept was critical in helping her reach her academic and personal goals at the same time.

As a fellow competitive runner in the Washington D.C. area, I met Vanessa over ten years ago. At the time, we were both new to marathon running. Another common interest was writing, and we each had established blogs to document our journeys. I was thrilled when Vanessa told me that she was writing a book. Having gone through the process of writing my own book, *Boston Bound*, I knew that Vanessa would find the experience truly rewarding.

Running has taught me larger life lessons. Of course, this was not my intent when I took up the sport back in 2005. I started running because I liked to challenge myself and set goals that were objective and not based on the perception of others. Running road races filled my desire to feel accomplished. But the honeymoon phase did not last long. I soon realized that not every race was going to be satisfying and that my body wasn't always going to perform at the level I expected it to. And, like everything in life, I couldn't control things like the weather, or getting injured—roadblocks that would prevent me from reaching my goals.

I had found a vehicle by which to learn and apply "life skills" that I didn't develop when I was growing up. Things like patience, resilience, positivity in the face of adversity, and tolerance for imperfection. In order to meet my goal of qualifying for the Boston Marathon, I had to learn these skills and apply them to the process of my training. And it wasn't easy. But I was a hard worker, dead set on getting to Boston, so I did learn these skills over time. Once I did, Boston was the icing on the cake. The real accomplishment was changing my mindset and becoming a happier person.

While running was a major source of anxiety in my life for several years, for Vanessa, it was her outlet. Training for a marathon while also pursuing her doctorate degree gave her much-needed balance and perspective. It gave her confidence. Readers with long-term goals that may seem daunting will benefit from reading Vanessa's story. She shares her most personal struggles, insecurities, and fears and how she overcame them, one step at a time.

- Elizabeth Clor, author of *Boston Bound: A 7-Year Journey to Overcome Mental Barriers and Qualify for the Boston Marathon*

Preface

On the night of our daughter Lucy's first birthday, streamers, cake crumbs, and presents were strewn about the house, but it was the shiny balloon that grabbed Lucy's attention. As my husband Pat whacked the helium balloon, Lucy laughed harder than she ever had in her short life. She shrieked as we hit the balloon again and again: each time, the "thwack" noise sent her into another round of giggles. My stomach hurt from laughing - Lucy was so full of joy and delight. It was a marvelous sight to behold. We had made it through the first year of our daughter's life: an accomplishment by most standards, but even more so in the middle of a pandemic that brought the entire world to a standstill.

I was relishing how much Lucy enjoyed her birthday. Yet, I also had a thought that rushed through my head, something I had thought so often during Lucy's first year on this planet: "I would've missed this."

Because years before, in the midst of a grueling grad school program, when I had lost all confidence in myself, I had recurring dark thoughts that kept me stuck in a depressive state. I did my best to hide these ideas from the outside world, trying to present myself as confident and positive. Inside, I was crumbling: filled with doubt and an inability to see myself getting through this dark abyss.

I am one of the lucky ones. With the support of family, friends, and a professional therapist and medication, I was able to get on the other side of this. But I know that these traits can be genetic, and therefore Lucy is likely to experience them as well. I want her to know that she's not alone, nor has she been the first to experience these feelings in her family.

There is so much that I need to teach Lucy. One of the most important lessons is that life is a marathon, not a sprint, and that there are so many people cheering her on every step of the way.

This story is for you, Lucy.

Introduction

"The miracle isn't that I had finished. The miracle is that
I had the courage to start." – John Bingham, author of
The Courage to Start: A Guide to Running for Your Life

On the surface, everything looked great in October 2015.
I was happily married, I was a multi-marathon finisher, I had
a loving family, and was in the midst of earning my Ph.D. Yet,
I was anxiously tapping my foot in a psychiatrist's office. I was
teetering on the precipice and in desperate need of help.

"Vanessa, was yesterday's panic attack the first one you've
ever had, or has this happened before?" asked Dr. Turner. As I
spoke to my psychiatrist about how my anxiety made me feel
like I was spiraling out of control, she pushed me to consider
the ways in which this episode was part of a larger pattern. Although I didn't have my college journal on hand, I knew there
was written evidence that showed that my anxiety was not only
interwoven with my experience in a rigorous doctoral program,
but had hovered over me like a dark shadow for years.

***

October 1, 2004

*I am tired beyond belief and yet I can't sleep. For the past two
nights, I have gotten a combined total of eight hours of sleep. But
when I get back to my room between classes to take a nap, I can't
sleep. I do not know how I am going to be able to survive like this.*

*I am also very stressed. I think I've had two panic attacks in
the past two days. My heart is racing all the time, even when I'm trying to nap.*

*I don't know how much longer I can go on like this. I don't
think I'm really happy anymore. I keep trying to throw myself into*

activities in order to not deal with the other stuff. My parents want me to do really well, but they don't want me to go over the edge. Before I went to college, my mom told me how a childhood friend had a brother who killed himself because he was afraid to tell his parents about his grades. She shared this story as a cautionary tale and an explicit reminder that my parents love me know matter what grades I get.

My stress keeps building up, and I don't know how I am going to figure this out.

Did I really make the right choice going here? Or am I slowly killing myself with everything going on here?

I have no idea what I am going to do. All I want is to be happy.

***

I had spent less than two months at The College of the Holy Cross when I wrote that anxious entry in the leatherbound diary all incoming students received on our first day of college. That passage represented an early marker of clinical anxiety - something that became a defining factor of my life in higher education. As I sought to advance through the university ranks in pursuit of a doctorate, I repeatedly felt like an imposter and worried that my attempts at success would fall short of my high aspirations. Not only did I struggle to adjust to college, I also feared that the sacrifices my family made for me were all for nothing.

***

I was born and raised in Spencerport, a small suburban town outside of Rochester, NY. Our charming little village reminded me of the fictitious town of Stars Hollow in "Gilmore Girls," complete with a gazebo in the center of town. It was a close-knit community filled with loving friends and family, at the center of which were our parents. As long as I can remember, my parents, Doug and Judy, worked tirelessly to give me and my younger sibling, Nova, better lives than they could have ever imagined for their own.

Whenever I think about what my mom, I usually imagine her working in the kitchen. The kitchen table was where we did our homework, which often meant she sat next to us, quizzing us on our multiplication tables and vocabulary flashcards. Sometimes she rose to tend to our dinner, other times, she checked our family calendar to write down the details about a birthday party or an upcoming field trip. Mom stayed at home with us until Nova went to first grade. She then became a reading specialist at our elementary school, but was always be there to greet us when we got off the bus at the end of the day. On Saturdays, while Nova and I went to our sports and music practices, she washed the floors and vacuumed. Our chore requirements were minimal, as both she and my dad wanted us to prioritize our schoolwork.

My dad, the operations manager of a local trucking company, left for work at 4:45 every morning, only to return long after we had finished dinner. He did not complain about working hard. This wasn't because he stepped into an environment that recognized his labors. I knew this first-hand when I worked in his office one summer during high school. Regularly, I saw people lose their tempers, throwing their arms up in frustration if a shipment was late getting out, no matter how hard Dad worked to manage the drivers. He often stayed late, making changes to a large whiteboard, trying to optimize the drivers' time, in an effort to make everyone's day more bearable. It was like watching Sisyphus pushing the boulder up every day. His work did not offer personal satisfaction - it was a means to an end.

When the weekend arrived, Dad happily threw himself into our weekend activities, even though I'm sure he hoped to catch up on sleep. He went on camping trips with Nova's scout troop or chaperoned my choir rehearsals. Work wasn't an escape from our family: being with us was what sustained him through those long hours. Because he had a commercial trucking license, he occasionally took overnight drives to pick up a shipment from Maine or New York City. Those long-hauls offered a hefty bonus that went to home repairs, occasionally a family vacation, or later on, our college tuition.

The day I got into Holy Cross, a small, competitive, liberal arts college in Worcester, Massachusetts, was one of the happiest days of my young life. Raised in the Catholic faith, I was eager to go to a college run by the Jesuits, a Catholic religious order that prioritized education, interreligious dialogue, and social justice. Yet, within a few weeks of arriving, I began to question if the admissions office had made a mistake in admitting me. Knowing how much my parents sacrificed so I could go to college made my first semester all the more stressful. The stakes felt high, and I feared I'd flunk out of school.

***

Since I did well in AP Calculus in high school, I foolishly enrolled in Calculus during my first semester at Holy Cross to complete my core math requirement. This intensive math class meant for STEM students confounded me at every turn. The professor held daily office hours, during which a group of us sat at a table and worked on our homework. Afraid of asking too many questions and looking like an idiot, I anxiously waited for my classmates to raise their hands, hoping they would eventually cave and ask the question that I also had. Then, I hastily scribbled down the professor's recommendations: hoping that her insights might finally penetrate my thick skull. Although my math grades in high school were decent, I had apparently reached my ceiling when it was time to tackle derivatives and integrals. I couldn't crack above a C on any test. Immensely discouraged, I hoped that my history classes could serve as both a diversion from the enormous difficulty of calculus, as well as a way to boost my overall GPA.

Even since my Girl Scout troop visited Susan B. Anthony's house in 4th grade and I learned about the women's suffrage movement, I knew I wanted to study history in college. I planned to then go onto law school and become a lawyer – what I thought of as the "practical" career for a history major. In the middle of September, I turned in my first college assignment: a five-page paper analyzing Aztec accounts of the Spanish conquest of Mexico. I had worked diligently on it all week, even staying up until 2 a.m. the night before to proofread it. As history was always my best subject in high school, I didn't even think there was reason to be nervous when the professor handed back the papers. Yet, my heart sank as I flipped to the final page, which contained a series of handwritten comments and the grade: C+.

I quickly shoved the paper in my notebook, hoping no one saw it. What did it mean if I was struggling this badly in the subject I loved the most? Was I completely out of my depth? My classmates seemed calm and collected. Most of them came from prep schools - was that why they were doing so much better? No one else seemed to be worrying about money, grades, fitting in, and the other litany of concerns that kept me up in the middle of the night.

I was convinced that my scholarship was in jeopardy. I felt panicked whenever I thought of going to class. How could I tell my parents, who had sacrificed so much for me to attend my dream school, that I was in danger of failing out? I'd fake a tone of optimism whenever I called my parents, saying, "Yes, things are busy, and the classes are hard, but I'm doing okay." Lies.

This anxiety culminated in a horrible week in the middle of the semester, when I had either a paper or test due in every single class. I was doing everything wrong: staying up late, drinking too much caffeine, and not exercising. Moreover, I bottled up my anxiety. Afraid to tell a single person, I wrote in my journal the painful entry that opens this chapter. I was plagued with insecurity and struggled to have any semblance of a normal sleep schedule.

When I was little and had trouble sleeping, I woke my parents up in a panic, crying, "I can't sleeeeep." Every time, even if he had to get up in a few hours to go to work, Dad came into my room and helped me fall back to sleep. He'd rub my back, and with a gentle, soothing voice, say, "Think about the beach, think about the soft sand under your feet, and think about the waves crashing on the shore. Shh..." Eventually, this calmed me down enough to drift off to sleep. But when I arrived at Holy Cross, I found no such relief.

I'd wake up in the middle of the night and remain awake for hours, my mind racing and heart pounding. It felt hard to breathe and I didn't know how to calm myself down. Sometimes I watched TV or read. Other times, I lay in bed, unable to relax enough to fall back asleep. More often than not, I decided to just get up and study, even though I clearly was not firing on all cylinders. I chalked up the stress to adjusting to college life. I didn't realize that not everyone was consumed by anxiety.

One night, as I was returning to my room after a night in the library, I heard my dorm phone ringing as I was unlocking my door. The answering machine picked up, "Hey Vanessa, it's Kathleen. I wanted to see how you're doing. I know it's your first week of midterms…"

It was Kathleen, my best friend from home and the person I looked up to most in the world. We met during the school musicals, and although she was three years older than me, we instantly clicked. The age difference made us more like sisters than friends. I idolized her, and for good reason: she was class valedictorian, friendly, kind, and well-loved. Even when she went off to college, we stayed in touch, and the times when she came home to visit were some of my happiest memories of high school. I hung onto her every word when it came to learning about life in college, both in terms of schoolwork and what it was like to live away from home. And like a big sister, she was now calling to check up on me.

"Hey," I said breathlessly, "How's it going?" I tried to sound casual, but inside, I was relieved she called. I didn't want to tell my parents how bad things were, but I knew I could confide in Kathleen.

"Are you okay, Vanessa?" Kathleen asked, her voice filled with concern. "I hadn't heard from you in a while and wanted to make sure you weren't drowning in midterms." The dam broke and I started to cry. "Kathleen - this is so hard. I thought I was ready for college, but everyone seems to be smarter than me. They don't seem to need to study as much either. No matter how hard I work, it never feels good enough. I think Holy Cross made a mistake in admitting me."

"Sweetie, I wish I could be there to give you a hug," Kathleen said. "I remember my first semester, and I felt just like you. The first semester is the worst one. If you can get through this one, everything else will be easier in comparison. I promise. I wouldn't lie to you, okay? You will get through midterms. I hate seeing you beat yourself like this. You are incredibly smart, and have earned the right to be there." These were comforting words, but by the next math class, Kathleen's advice had slipped away.

I couldn't reconcile the fact that my dream school had turned into a nightmare. Attending my math professor's office hours felt pointless: I wasn't showing any improvement. In visiting the library's Writing Center, I received some guidance to help improve my history papers. Still, I worried that those initial poor grades would weigh down my overall GPA.

When my parents picked me up at the train station for Thanksgiving break, they eyed me warily. I had bags under my eyes, and even through my cable knit sweater, it was evident that I had lost weight: a pretty big deal for someone who weighed less than 100 pounds. But they didn't say anything to show their concern: instead, they just hugged me. Worn out from the travel and the past three months, I went to bed immediately. I was relieved to be in my own bed, and gave in to the overwhelming sense of exhaustion. I didn't head downstairs the next day until almost noon: a stark difference from all of the years when I was first at the table for breakfast.

While Mom and Dad watched me as I poured my coffee, my stomach filled with dread at the impending conversation. Implicit in how they raised us was that they wanted Nova and I to take advantage of every available opportunity, especially those that were not afforded to them. I was failing to make their sacrifices worthwhile.

Cautiously, my parents asked, "how are your classes going?" I immediately burst into tears. "I'm going to fail!" All of the tension and stress that I had kept under lock and key all semester erupted in a fit of crying. Mom and Dad asked what I was doing to get help, and while I said I was going to office hours, I added, "It's not working!" Nothing they said could calm me down. It made for a tense Thanksgiving break. I tried to relax with my family. However, after a few hours, I went upstairs to work on my final papers, hoping that this Hail Mary attempt would prevent me from getting kicked out of Holy Cross.

The rest of the semester, I studied in a beaten-up study carrel in the library: trying to extract as much as I could from my textbooks and copious notes. Once I got on the train for the 9-hour ride home for Christmas, I fell asleep, relieved to be done with the semester, yet uncertain about my final grades.

It wasn't until the grades finally arrived a few days before Christmas that I, along with my parents, let out a huge sigh of relief. I had managed to get a C+ in calculus. Not great, but passable. My other grades were mildly better. I was not going to fail out of college or lose my scholarship. While my first semester was rough, it turned out to be my worst academic semester of my collegiate career. I knew which classes to avoid (I never took a math class again), and how to better set myself up for success. I mentally pushed those first panic attacks aside and chalked them up to the stress of adjusting to college.

***

It was a gray morning when I shuffled into my favorite class: a history seminar on the Black Death. Our class was taught by a Jesuit priest named Fr. Worcester, who, when he lectured, spoke with a deep baritone voice that reminded me of James Earl Jones. That morning, he made a passing comment before the start of class about getting ready to present his latest research at a conference, which immediately piqued our interest. Knowing we had some time before we began our discussion, we peppered Fr. Worcester with questions about his research and what his life looked like as a professor. Delaying the formal start of class for twenty minutes, Fr. Worcester spoke passionately about writing his doctoral dissertation, conducting archival research, and the joys of teaching. *Wait, I could spend my entire career reading and writing about history? Instead of my passion being limited to my college major, it could be the central focus of my life's work?*

While my classmates found it to be a fascinating discussion, I walked out feeling electrified. Unknowingly, Fr. Worcester altered the course of my professional life that day. No longer would I go to law school, as I had planned for years. I was told that was the "sensible" thing to do as a history major. Instead, I decided that I too wanted to pursue a doctorate and spend my career researching and teaching. I wanted to get students interested in history as my professors had for me. This initial excitement fueled me during the rest of my time at Holy Cross: all of my academic decisions became centered on gaining admittance to graduate school.

***

I had settled into an academic routine at Holy Cross, and focused on honing my writing and research skills to put me on a path to becoming a medieval historian. Even though my high school history classes quickly passed through the Middle Ages, a course at Holy Cross opened my eyes to this interesting and complex period. Three days a week, we explored different socio-religious movements, as well as how some of the medieval cultural and political legacies have had a lasting impact on our own world. In addition to reading the vivid written narratives from the period, I loved examining the beautiful pieces of art, music, and literature as ways to illuminate what seemed to be a distant world.

As my senior year approached, I applied for and was accepted into the history department's honors program, which culminated in a year-long thesis project. I had found published records from a trial in 1324 about a woman named Alice Kyteler who was accused of killing three of her husbands and breaking into a church at night to perform illicit rituals with a group of women. The salacious court records were fascinating to read, and offered a unique window to understanding some of the misogynistic portrayals of women in the Middle Ages.

I worked closely with my advisor, Professor Lorraine Attreed, who mentored me throughout my time at Holy Cross. She coached me as I prepared to present a paper at my first academic conference, and offered her insights about possible grad school programs to consider. We met weekly to talk about my thesis, usually focusing on the most recent batch of pages I had submitted. As I sat in her office, surrounded by hundreds of books about the Middle Ages, I thought that academically, I couldn't be happier. I had finally settled into a groove at Holy Cross and found an area of research that captured my imagination. I had received an acceptance letter from The Catholic University of America, whose history department was well-known for their excellence in medieval history. The thesis represented the culmination of my hard work, and offered proof to both me and the history department that I was prepared to do advanced work as a graduate student.

When it was time to present my thesis in May, Professor Attreed proudly sat in the front row, beaming as I outlined the scope of my project. With a sense of relief, I submitted my 137-page thesis to the department for review. Based on the feedback I received from Professor Attreed, I felt confident about the outcome.

During Senior Week, that final fun week of activities between classes and graduation, I checked my email before getting ready for our class picnic. My heart sank as I quickly scanned the message from the department,

Dear Vanessa,

We have reviewed your thesis, and while you presented some fascinating material, you did not meet the standards of the History Honors Program. Therefore, you will not be granted departmental honors at graduation. We do think you have the potential to grow as a historian and wish you all the best as you begin your new life after Holy Cross.

The History Honors Committee

I was stunned. There were no warnings that this was happening. I quickly wrote to Professor Attreed to ask if we could meet the following day to discuss what happened. I washed my face (which turned red and my eyes were swollen from shedding a few tears) and got ready to go out with my friends. I was too mortified to tell my classmates, even my closest friends. Instead, I drowned my disappointment in white wine. While everyone else also was drinking heavily, their imbibing was out of celebration: mine was in defeat.

The next day, I sat slightly hungover in Professor Attreed's office, the place which had given me so much joy all year, to see if there was anything she could do to appeal this decision. Looking at me solemnly, she shook her head no. I could see that this was a painful experience for her as well. She then went on to talk about some of the concerns that the committee voiced, but ultimately stressed, "You still have it in you to go onto grad school. Please don't give up on your larger goal."

Despite these words of wisdom, I remained ashamed. My parents they made it clear that it in no way tarnished the fact that I was graduating from college. In particular, my mom underscored this point, as she was never able to go to college herself: "Vanessa, you're achieving more than I was ever able to academically: your father and I are so proud of you," she said lovingly. But to me, graduation felt tainted.

My final transcript did not set off any alarm bells at Catholic. However, my insecurities were great enough to begin with that I did not want to give the history department at any more ammunition to reconsider accepting me. In some ways, it felt like I ended my time at Holy Cross the same way I began: unsure whether I deserved to be there in the first place.

That dark cloud of self-doubt continued to follow me throughout all of grad school.

Chapter 1: Standing on the Starting Line

"I am about to make a transition greater
in magnitude than any that I have made before.
How is my life about to change?"

Upon graduating from Holy Cross in 2008, I wrote one last entry in my college journal, responding to that final prompt about my life as a college student. Despite my insecurities lingering from the fallout over my senior thesis, I tried to feign optimism about this transitional moment.

***

May 26, 2008

It is my dream to become a medievalist who is published and respected in my field. I want students to enjoy taking my classes and to come to my office for guidance and assistance. I imagine an office full of books, images, and objects that are all indicative of my love of the Middle Ages. I want to get people excited about learning.

I suppose the most obvious example of how I'll act on my desires is by attending The Catholic University of America in the fall. I'll be studying medieval history under the tutelage of Professor Katherine Jansen – a woman whom I'm looking forward to meeting. We've talked on the phone a few times, and I think we made a good connection. I'm really going to have to bust my butt in grad school. But I'm excited about the program and looking forward to living in D.C. – that should be awesome.

***

It is not always clear when one is beginning a new adventure. Yet in other cases, the banners and pageantry are out on full display, and we are anxiously waiting to begin our journey.

When I moved to Washington D.C. in August 2008, it was

evident that I was standing at the starting line of a new race. Three months after graduating from college, I arrived at our nation's capital to begin a master's program at The Catholic University of America in medieval history. I did not know anyone in the Washington and this new phase of my life was uncharted territory.

The days leading up to the first day of school were a blur of orientation seminars, welcome receptions, and meetings. During these gatherings, I felt young, inexperienced, and lost. Barely five feet tall, a number of university officials welcomed me to "my freshman year at CUA," not realizing that I was a graduate student. Everyone was nice, yet I feared that I had a beacon over me that screamed, "I'm new! I'm confused! And I'm not entirely sure if I belong here!" I tried to shove these feelings aside as I smiled and shook the hands of each professor and administrator, drying my sweaty palms on my new dress in between handshakes.

The Friday before classes started, I met with Dr. Jim Riley, the department chair, a friendly senior professor who offered the kind smile of a grandfather, as well as some words of encouragement. Seeing my knee jiggle throughout our conversation, he sensed how nervous I was about starting this new endeavor. As he walked me out of the history department, I smacked my head into the glass door. Embarrassed, I turned around and joked, "You must keep this really clean," and shuffled out the door.

A most auspicious beginning.

***

When I started graduate school, I wanted to adopt some new healthy habits. Most importantly, I decided this was my opportunity to finally become a regular runner.

Growing up, I never considered myself to be athletic. After getting the wind knocked out of me in second-grade soccer, I tended to duck when any ball flew in my direction. My hands were best used when holding up a book.

When I began middle school, our P.E. teachers insisted that every student sign up for either soccer or cross-country.

Given my failed soccer days in elementary school, I signed up for cross-country, much to the amusement of my parents. To this day, Mom loves to remind me that at the end of a long shopping trip at Greece Ridge Mall, I used to ask if she could bring the car around, in order to avoid the need to double back. Despite their well-founded skepticism, they supported my quest to take up this sport. During the summer of 1998, my mom drove me to the high school track a few mornings a week. Following the school's suggestion, I ran one mile around the track, huffing as my mom and Nova looked on from the bleachers. Wearing oversized soccer shorts that ballooned around my chicken legs, I enjoyed the solitude of completing my laps. Even though I wasn't that fast, finishing my mile each day brought a sense of accomplishment I had never felt in any other athletic activity.

Though I arrived on the first day of 7th grade cross-country practice not particularly speedy, I was in better shape than those who did not do any summer training. Following the "bang" of the starting pistol, we disappeared into the woods. My lack of sprint speed caused me to lag behind those who bolted right out of the gate. Heading into the forest, I trailed behind, nearly in last place during the first stretch of the race. Yet in the quiet and secrecy of the wooded paths, I made my move: slowly passing people throughout and emerging from the woods far ahead of what people expected from me. Although I was a middling performer, what I really enjoyed was the camaraderie of the team. Yet, when 9th grade came around, and cross-country practices conflicted with the opportunity to be in the school plays, I hung up my shoes and put this brief stint of athleticism into a box, to be packed away for years.

In high school, I threw myself into the performing arts: I sang, played clarinet, took piano lessons, and was in the annual musical. Aside from my studies, music was my life, and I took that love to college, singing in three classical groups, touring Italy and performing at Mass in St. Peter's Basilica. Athletes seemed to be a different breed. I gave off such a music vibe, that the idea that I would ever become a runner, let alone a marathoner, was surprising, even laughable, to my family and friends.

Eager to stave off the Freshman 15, I jogged 2-3 miles around the Holy Cross campus a couple of times a week. But as schoolwork inevitably picked up, I fell off the fitness wagon yet again. I tried to embody a healthy lifestyle in college, but ultimately, I prioritized academics over both exercise and sleep.

The only time I ever truly tried to stretch the limits of my running abilities in college was when I ran with Fr. Michael McFarland. The college president had a blanket offer that he would run with any student who asked. Eager to spend a little one-on-one time with the person whose Sunday homilies I enjoyed, I took him up on his offer, thinking we would cover about three miles. However, when I showed up in front of the Jesuit residence at 6 a.m. on a Wednesday morning, he asked, "Is five miles okay? I have a great loop around campus and Worcester that I think you'd enjoy." I balked, having never run so far in my life. I blurted out, "Sure, that would be great!" As we climbed the hills of Worcester, Fr. McFarland told me about his experiences running the fabled Boston Marathon: the prestigious race that required all of its entrants to run a qualifying time in order to participate. Because of Worcester's proximity to Boston, I was acutely aware of Patriots' Day, also known as Marathon Monday – the third Monday in April when the fastest runners in the country converged in Hopkinton, Massachusetts to begin their 26.2-mile pilgrimage to Boston. I asked questions about the race that I knew required long answers, in hopes of conserving oxygen as I struggled to keep up with his pace. Despite the fact that Fr. McFarland was in his mid-fifties, he was in excellent shape, and ran with an unmatchable ease.

At the end of the run, I thanked him for taking time out of his busy schedule, and then hobbled back to my dorm room. Although this route was his usual midweek workout, it was the longest and hardest run I had ever completed. I was sore for days: I felt like I had been run over by a truck. From that point,

I viewed five miles as a distance that I did not think I could ever complete again.

When I moved to D.C. a year later, I vowed to make a change. I thought that running regularly could be a good coping mechanism for graduate school. It would keep me in shape and help alleviate the stress that I anticipated could emerge during graduate school.

With the feeling of optimism that one has when making a New Year's resolution, I decided to go for a run around campus the day before classes started. As I ran on the sidewalk alongside parents moving in their children, splat! I wiped out. To my surprise and disappointment, *no one helped me up*. This was *The* Catholic University of America - weren't people supposed to be charitable? Bleeding with two skinned knees, scraped palms, and a bruised ego, I sheepishly shuffled back to my dorm room. Between walking into the glass door in front of the department chair and face-planting on my run, I was proving to be quite a klutz on campus. I had planned to wear sundresses for the first week of school, but I didn't want to look like a hot mess with band aids everywhere. Instead, I opted for dress pants, and sweated my way, literally, through those first few classes in the late August heat. My skinned knees healed, and I cautiously took to the campus roads again, gingerly stepping into my new life.

***

On my first day of "Medieval Women, Sex, and Gender," I filed into the classroom, grabbing an empty desk in the circle. Then the more advanced students entered, happily chatting amongst themselves about what they did over the summer. A tall guy that I recognized from orientation took the seat next to me and said with a smile, "Hi, I'm Wes." Wes was a new doctoral student and I was grateful that he had made the effort to introduce himself. I quickly found out he'd be in my other history courses that semester. Even though he had already earned a master's degree, he was also new to Catholic. I was thankful that someone else would be going through this adjustment process alongside me.

After a few minutes, Dr. Katherine Jansen, the Princeton-educated professor who I came to Catholic to study with, entered the room. She had perfectly coiffed copper-red hair, and a voice that resonated with the joy of Julia Child mixed with the gravitas of Christine Baranski. As she took attendance, she looked around the room, happily greeting her returning students, and then finally got to my name. I meekly raised my hand. "Oh, *you're* Vanessa Taylor," Dr. Jansen intoned, giving me a warm smile. "It's nice to finally meet you. Welcome to Catholic University."

Although I loved the assigned reading, with books that discussed medieval nuns, powerful queens, and what motherhood was like in the Middle Ages, I was overwhelmed by the class discussions. I was the lone new medieval graduate student that year. While I had recently turned 22, the students were in their late 20s, 30s, and even on the other side of 40. I felt young and naïve among the more seasoned students. They were more put together in every respect, wearing Ralph Lauren and Banana Republic, whereas my fanciest outfits came from The Gap. They were more financially secure: when a group of us went out to dinner, they were always eager to order both appetizers *and* drinks, never flinching when the bill came. I always felt a step behind, both in and out of the classroom.

During the two-hour seminar each week, I tried to come up with noteworthy contributions to the discussion, attempting to impress Dr. Jansen. She was intimidating: her reputation as an eminent scholar of late medieval religious history was well-known throughout campus.

Not only did Dr. Jansen demand excellence, she also didn't suffer fools. One time in the middle of a class presentation, a student admitted she didn't know one of the main points of content that was the subject of her own report. Dr. Jansen dryly interjected, "Haven't you ever heard of a little thing called Wikipedia?" causing the class to burst into laughter. Funny as that was, that remark caused me to make sure I always walked into discussion well-prepared and able to discuss every aspect of the material.

The more senior students seemed so sure of themselves. They always responded to Dr. Jansen's questions confidently and with long, detailed answers. I, on the other hand, struggled to get out more than a couple of coherent sentences about the week's reading assignment. Wes, who had already gone through a master's program, told me, "Don't worry, you're doing fine. You have to remember that not everyone who is talking all of the time in class says something meaningful. Sometimes they're only talking to talk. You'll get the hang of it." As we packed up our books, Wes invited me to get lunch with some of the other history students. It was a welcome relief from reading alone in the cafeteria. Because of Wes's initial act of kindness, I started to feel less alone.

***

As my academic advisor, Dr. Jansen was responsible for monitoring my progress as a graduate student. Midway through the semester, she emailed all of her students that we were to schedule a check-in with her. Although the meeting was routine, I worried that I wasn't demonstrating my full potential at Catholic.

I had recently developed a nervous habit of keeping a mint in my mouth, sometimes chewing on several during class to help me relax. But as I checked my purse before heading out to my meeting, I discovered that the Altoid tin was empty. *Shoot*, I thought to myself. While I was brushing my teeth, I noticed in my medicine cabinet that I had a bag of cough drops leftover from a cold. I grabbed a couple, putting one in my mouth as I went to the library. Walking over to her office later that afternoon, I took a second one. When I checked in at the front desk, the administrative assistant said Dr. Jansen was running across campus from another meeting. As I waited for her, I took my third cough drop of the day. Dr. Jansen walked in, full of apologies, then invited me to sit down.

I presented to her a list of courses I was thinking of taking in the spring, all of which she approved. Dr. Jansen asked a few questions about how my other classes were going, and then she paused, causing my heart to race. She lowered her thick tortoise-shell glasses, peering over the lenses at me with a puzzled look, "Vanessa, are you sick? I think I can smell menthol."

What could I say to her? *No, I'm not sick, I'm just nervous and I thought that sucking on cough drops was apparently a good coping mechanism.* Instead, I meekly replied, "Uh, yeah. I'm getting over a cold." It was a flat-out lie: I was perfectly healthy. "Well, if you've got nothing else to report, I'm going to ask if you wouldn't mind heading out. I'm flying out to a conference this weekend and I don't want to get whatever you have," she said, matter-of-factly. I thanked her for her time, and then quickly shuffled out of her office.

I went to the Starbucks on campus, where Wes and the other history students worked and socialized. "How did it go?" they asked, knowing that I had been fretting about the meeting. I told them about the cough drop incident. They all burst out laughing. "Vanessa, that's ridiculous! Why didn't you tell her you were nervous?" they asked. I shook my head. "No! I'd rather have her think I'm sick." Although they thought it was hysterical, it was a prime example of how my nerves interfered with school.

***

Because Latin was the primary written language used across Western Europe for nearly a millennium, it is expected that all medievalists become proficient in the language. When I arrived at Catholic, I only had one semester of Latin under my belt from Holy Cross. I knew a reckoning awaited me as I sought to learn a language that was integral to my field.

The only thing that made intensive Latin tolerable was that Wes was also part of this baptism by fire. Three days a week, we met at 8 a.m. at Starbucks for what I dubbed "Latin Matin Mania." With our English-Latin dictionaries, translation assignments, and declension charts spread out over two tables, we put our heads together as we sought to decipher Cicero and Ovid. All of this was meant to prepare us for the culminating moment a few hours later when Professor Patel called on us at random to read a section of the translation.

My concentration broke whenever the professor interrupted to say "what declension" or "conjugate this to past perfect
tense." I froze: all of the knowledge I had amassed hours before
crumbled. I turned into a sputtering mess.

"Vanessa, it's going to get easier," Wes said to me after
class, knowing how dejected I was about my latest performance.
I appreciated his support, but couldn't get behind his optimism
about my ability to grasp the language, as my middling grades
proved otherwise.

***

Not only was I anxious about fitting in at Catholic, I was
dealing with a great deal of uncertainty in my personal life. I was
trying to untangle myself from my college boyfriend, Matthew.
We had met in choir practice during our first year of college, and
the beginning period was filled with all of the simple joys of a
first relationship. Those first dates and kisses all felt carefree.

But after a few months of dating, I was conforming to
Matthew's expectations of what it meant to be a good girlfriend,
while not holding him to any similar standard. We spent more
time with his friends than mine. While I made an effort to get
to know Matthew's parents, he remained aloof and closed-off
any time my parents came to visit. He always acted like it was a
burden to be with the people who were most important to me.
My parents had raised me to be a force of nature, but I shrunk
to make himself feel big. What was I thinking? That no one else
could like me? Was I that insecure that I thought it was better to
settle?

Each of those red flags individually should've been problematic enough for me to dump him. But I couldn't find a way
out. For all of the benefits of a small liberal arts school, the
ultimate downside was that any breakup immediately became
campus fodder. I saw other couples split up on our small campus, and the proximity was such that it was often awkward
for the rest of their time in college. Another choir couple broke
up, and they always looked miserable during rehearsals. I didn't

want the same thing to happen. Somehow, I was willing to tolerate Matthew's problematic behavior instead of dealing with a temporary sense of discomfort. I felt trapped.

One night, a bunch of our mutual friends got together to play board games on what should have been a forgettable Saturday evening. Despite my best efforts, when it was my turn to guess whatever clue he was acting out in Charades, I could not get the right answer. Matthew's volatile explosion was not that of an overly-competitive person, but of someone whose anger went beyond the scope of the game. "Folks, it's only a game," one of my friends chimed in, jumping to my defense, "I couldn't have guessed it either." Matthew shot me dirty looks for the rest of the evening, as if my entire value was wrapped up in this inconsequential game. As we packed up for the night, one of my friends hugged me goodbye and whispered in my ear, "Are you okay?" "Yeah, I'm fine," I responded, "He just gets overly competitive." As I had done on multiple occasions, I was defending behavior that I would've found to be problematic in anyone else's significant other. And yet, months turned into years together. Time passing only made me feel more stuck. Yet, the reasons to walk away kept piling up.

Regardless of the subject: pop culture, social issues, or politics, Matthew's opinions became dogma. He was unwilling to ever concede a point. One semester, when we took a class together, and I scored better on an assignment than he did, he refused to speak to me for the rest of the day. "You only got an A because you're a suck-up," he said before initiating the silent treatment, as if I couldn't possibly have the intellectual capability of ever surpassing him. When we both applied for the same promotion and I got the job over him, he drank heavily all weekend, silently resenting my accomplishment. I had the perfect excuse - *this* was time to end it. Yet, I didn't walk away from Matthew, despite the fact that he could never celebrate anything that put me ahead of him. I had shrunk myself down to make him feel big.

I knew it was bad because I was lying to everyone about

the relationship. My friends at Holy Cross had a front-row seat to his behavior, but to everyone from Rochester, they saw pictures of us on Facebook that made us look like a happy couple. Even though I had clued Kathleen into a few of our fights in the beginning of our relationship, I started to share less and less. Those omissions were telling: Kathleen was the person I told everything. I was embarrassed to tell her about Matthew's outbursts - I knew she would've told me to break up with him. That should've been another clue that I needed to end it.

Matthew kept seeking ways to control my life, and I didn't know how to draw boundaries. One time, as I logged into my email, Matthew asked for my password. Without thinking, I told him. When I requested that Matthew reciprocate, he refused. He had complete access to my life, but clearly wanted to keep his own walls up. I was so bothered by it, but I didn't know how to say, "No. Some things are meant to be kept private." Instead, he read emails from my professors and family: everything from the mundane to the personal. When we graduated and no longer used a Holy Cross email address, I refused to grant him access to my new account. It was the smallest form of resistance, but also yet another indication that this relationship was problematic.

When it was time to think about graduate school, we applied to some schools in the same cities. However, when I chose to go to D.C. for grad school, which ultimately put me hundreds of miles away from Matthew, I thought to myself, "Maybe this will finally fizzle out and we can chalk it up to the long distance." During that first year, we visited each other on occasion, though the gaps in communication became longer and longer. Still, I couldn't pull the trigger and break up with him. Instead, we limped on. As overwhelming as it was to begin graduate school, it was a timely distraction from what had become a troublesome relationship.

***

Because I only had a partial scholarship to CUA, I worked part-time as an assistant director of one of the residential communities on campus. My supervisor, Joyce Milling, greeted me with open arms and regularly invited me over for dinner – a welcome break from dining hall food. I enjoyed socializing with her and her husband Charlie, who had just begun graduate school as well. When Charlie heard that I was getting into running, he invited me to join him on his Saturday morning runs. Each Saturday, we watched the sunrise as we ran around the monuments. On our runs we talked about everything: adjusting to grad school, religion, TV, and living in D.C.

By October, I managed to get out the door at least four days a week. Running offered me a feeling of normalcy and gave a semblance of structure that I craved. Even when Charlie and I were only running five miles, we believed that we could do anything. We were so bold in our dreaming that we said we could one day complete a marathon.

One morning I opened an email from Charlie. He said that we had been running long enough and that we should give the marathon a shot. "Vanessa, The National Marathon is five months away: we should do it," Charlie wrote enthusiastically. With hardly a moment's hesitation, I replied in all-capitals, "YES!" It sounded like such a big adventure to take on, and I was excited to try something outside of my comfort zone. The next weekend, we ran our longest run ever – six miles through Rock Creek Park. Even though it was less than a quarter of the 26.2-mile distance of the marathon, we were eager to increase our mileage. As the weather became cooler, our runs gradually extended into the double digits.

Although I was full of apprehension about how I was doing as a graduate student, the marathon training gave me a boost of excitement and added a little spring in my step. One day, as we were walking to class together, Dr. Jansen, asked with concern reminiscent of my parents, how I was getting settled in and whether I was making any friends. Feeling more confident than usual, I told her that I had decided to train for a marathon. "Good for you!" she responded enthusiastically, "Physical fitness is so important during graduate school, particularly when you're sitting around reading and researching. This is great."

She ultimately became one of the greatest advocates of my new-found hobby.

***

I found a beginner's marathon plan online that gradually increased my endurance. My attempt to develop a running habit mirrored my efforts to get settled into graduate school. Both endeavors involved early mornings, coffee, and stretching myself to push harder and work more toward a bigger goal. I was learning so much about myself as I settled into this new phase of my life. Seeking to document this new journey, I created a blog entitled, "Medievalist Running in Circles."

***

December 11, 2008

I am almost 2 months into my marathon training, and wanted to share my progress, since now people keep asking how the training is going. I kept a diary when I was 6, in middle school, and then in college, but I'd like to keep up a regular writing habit – something I hope will help me write my dissertation someday.

***

The blog served as a measuring chart of both my running and academic progress. It was as if someone measured my growth and marked it on the wall each year. If I felt I had reached a plateau in my performance, I could return to earlier entries to remind myself of my progress: both the low points and growth spurts. As I got into blogging, I discovered an online running community that connected me with runners all over the world. Hundreds of people regularly read and commented on my blog. Their comments offered the reassurance that others had overcome similar challenges, which made me feel more hopeful.

***

Seeking to test our fitness, Charlie and I signed up for my first official road race: the Jingle All the Way 10k - one of the city's most popular road races. Looking back, I was completely unprepared for my first formal race on December 14, 2008. I had the endurance to complete the 6.2-mile race but made mistakes throughout the race. We scrambled to find parking and sprinted to make it to the start line on time. I was stunned to see over 4,500 runners who were ready to run at 8 a.m., many of whom wore holiday apparel: dressed as Santa, reindeer, and an assortment of other holiday figures. At registration, they handed out jingle bells, which we tied to our shoelaces. When we set off, it sounded like a massive sleigh was slowly making its way around Hains Point. I had no sense of the time, as I was wearing a Mickey Mouse analog watch, whose hands offered no real indication of pacing. I proudly wore the red cotton race t-shirt, which I later learned shows that you're a novice runner, unlike the veteran racers, who wore technical apparel in a rainbow display of fluorescent tops and spandex-like shorts and tights.

The beginning of the race was congested, and after the starting siren went off, people hopped up onto the curb, jockeying for a better position. It felt like the entrance to a Black Friday sale. Feeling behind, I tried to weave my way through the crowds (looking back, that was a huge waste of time – you lose energy by doing this). Charlie and I picked up the pace at the halfway point, as I realized I could go a bit faster. As I got settled into a better position, I surveyed the other runners, all who were enjoying themselves. People were out running because they liked it, not because it was an extracurricular activity that looked good on college applications. This felt different from my middle school cross-country races, when I was a bundle of nerves. I was enjoying this! Finding one last gear inside, I charged ahead, my arms pumping to get me to the finish line.

Time: 55:04

Pace: 8:52/mile

Division (Women 20-24): 110/325

Overall women: 533/2,114

I had finished my first road race and I was hooked. As I later noted in my blog, "If running a 10k was that enjoyable, imagine how completing a marathon will feel."

Chapter 2: Finding My Footing

"The marathon can humble you." – Bill Rodgers,
Four-time winner of the Boston Marathon

I flew home to Rochester a few hours after the race, feeling relieved about completing my first semester of graduate school. My history grades were fine, although both professors noted that my writing needed some improvement. The B- I earned in Latin was not ideal, but at least it meant I could advance to the next level. Trying to put the grade past me, I was excited about a real break from school. It was a relief to not wake up at the crack of dawn every morning to do Latin translations and to not go to bed at night fretting about my preparedness for the daily quizzes that awaited me. I was eager to go home and spend a couple of weeks with my parents and Nova.

I was almost four years old when Nova was born, thus ending my short reign as an only child. I'm not proud to admit that I was not always a great big sister. I was jealous of the attention they got as a child, and as mortified as I am to acknowledge it, my jealousy even manifested itself at their own birthday parties. We fought like many siblings: getting overly competitive when playing board games, or arguing over who got to pick the next activity. I was more introverted, and eagerly retreated to my room to read, while Nova just wanted a playmate. However, when our interests aligned, we'd amuse ourselves for hours on end.

One of the happiest moments of our childhood was our first trip to Disney World. As we walked around the Magic Kingdom on that first day, we kept saying "Thank you, thank you" to our parents: grateful that we had arrived at the place we had been dreaming of for months. My favorite picture from that trip is of the two of us hugging each other on the shuttle bus ride home from our first day at Disney. All of the superficial fights that tended to erupt had been forgotten: pushed aside while we enjoyed everything at the happiest place on earth. It was memories like those that we nostalgically recalled during that Christmas break.

***

Over the holiday break, I completed my longest run ever: 14 miles. According to my training plan, I was on track to successfully finish the marathon. After reading the book *Four Months to a Four-Hour Marathon*, I secretly made that my time goal. I was getting in some solid training, feeling like I was getting into decent shape, and was looking forward to completing long runs with Charlie when I returned for the spring semester.

While we were out on what was supposed to be a 14-mile run, Charlie hobbled to a halt less than two miles into our run, complaining of knee pain. Regretfully, he withdrew from the marathon a few days later.

I was sad to lose my running buddy, particularly because of the wonderful conversations we had on those chilly Saturday mornings. However, I was determined to continue in my quest to be a marathoner. Although I'm extroverted, I also appreciate having time to myself. Running gave me quiet time to unload my thoughts and plan for the day ahead.

That winter, running alone helped me learn my way around D.C. For my Saturday long runs, I ran up North Capitol Street, past Union Station, and around the National Mall. These runs took me by the Capitol, the Washington Monument, and then around the Lincoln Memorial. If I wanted to add in a few extra miles, I ventured across the Key Bridge into Virginia, running past the Arlington Cemetery. I was awestruck by D.C.'s rich history and beautiful monuments that made up its iconic skyline. Although most runs have blurred together in my mind, others, even more than a decade later, still remain vivid memories. I went for a long run around the National Mall the day before

President Barack Obama was sworn in. It was amazing to feel the energy in our nation's capital as the country readied itself for this historic moment.

On Tuesday January 20, 2009, I stood shivering on the National Mall with my friends as we waited for hours to witness Obama's inauguration. Somehow, standing alongside the roughly two million other spectators at 6 a.m., it didn't feel as cold. I was grateful that they replayed the "We are One" Inauguration Concert from the day before on the JumboTron, which offered some much-needed entertainment. As "Shout" by the Isley Brothers came on, we all jumped up and down, singing along "a little bit louder now," as if we were at a concert. The spirit of friendship and excitement that was part of this massive sea of humanity was an experience like no other.

As President Obama addressed the nation, he spoke about the challenges our country faced, noting that "We must be firm in the knowledge that there is nothing so satisfying to the spirit, so defining of our character, than giving our all to a difficult task." Whenever I was confronted with a seemingly insurmountable challenge, I returned to that memorable line for inspiration.

***

My runs became more routine that winter. I created a figure-eight loop around campus I used for the next decade: covering thousands of miles in all weather and seasons. The four-mile route, which I could run practically blindfolded, stretched around the perimeter of CUA, and went through the neighborhood of Brookland. The path was filled with long, rolling hills: perfect for training. If I wanted to stretch it out to eight miles, I ran the second loop in the opposite direction from the first. My favorite parts of the route were the times when I was able to glimpse the National Shrine, which was adjacent to Catholic's campus.

Unless it was an especially foggy day, The Basilica of the National Shrine of the Immaculate Conception stood as an enormous landmark throughout the run, with its spire pointed upward, like a finger beckoning toward the heavens. During my late afternoon runs, the fading rays glinted off the gold paint of the dome, adding an ethereal glow to the largest Roman Catholic Church in North America. There were different chapels within the shrine that I loved to visit, especially the one dedicated to Our Lady of Perpetual Help. Ahead of every exam, I ascended the marble steps to seek the Virgin Mary's guidance and support. This ritual offered a moment of quiet relief before each test. The shrine functioned as a silent witness to each challenge I sought to overcome in graduate school.

***

Each draining two-hour Latin class made me question why I was in love with medieval history, given that I had a hard time mastering the language that was required to study it. If I opted to specialize in modern European or American history, my years of studying French would've been sufficient.

Any Latin course is rigorous by design, but Professor Patel was tough. He opted to shame those of us who struggled, rather than offer encouragement. It's one thing to teach with a firm disposition, but to embarrass those who faltered was cruel. The hours leading up to each class were filled with dread. No amount of studying with Wes ever made me feel prepared. I often left class with my eyes brimming with tears. I felt embarrassed and frustrated with my lack of progress.

After I changed out of my dress clothes and into my workout attire, I took those emotions out on my runs. Even when I was feeling discouraged, I could slip on my running shoes and blow off steam, putting aside declensions and conjugations for an hour as I breathed in the fresh air. I relied on running to provide a physical and emotional release from the tumultuous aspects of my studies. In my head, I chased down my teacher, imagining my physical strength to be enough to vanquish his harsh comments. *I* was the one who had the endurance to run double-digit miles. Surely, Professor Patel's looks of condescension would disappear in a flash if he saw me running down the National Mall. I psyched myself up before Latin tests by listening to the *Rocky* "Gonna Fly Now" theme song, getting amped to prove him wrong.

It was a tactic that I learned to employ throughout graduate school.

***

As the marathon drew closer, the runs grew longer and harder. It took me three tries to get over the 15-mile hump: I felt completely sapped in those final miles. Each time I came up short, I'd take the metro home, feeling dejected about my inability to finish my intended mileage. I also worried that these failures signaled that I wouldn't be able to finish the marathon in March. Coupled with my poor grades in Latin, I felt that I was struggling to succeed on a number of fronts.

On a beautiful 50-degree day in the middle of February, I attempted once again to get past the 15-mile barrier. This time, I slowed my pace from the start, hoping to avoid another burnout. When I turned onto Michigan Avenue to hit the homestretch of my run, I could see my "finish line" – the National Shrine. Even after 14 miles, I still felt good. Excited that I was able to run for over two hours without stopping, I stretched the run to 16 miles. Although I felt victorious, I journaled about my apprehension about going the full distance of the marathon,

As exciting as that experience was, it is disconcerting to know that after 16 miles, I'll have more than 10 more miles to go on marathon day (exactly 6 weeks away). Right now, I feel as if I have the energy to go a few more miles, but 10? I'm not sure. Then again, I need to keep reminding myself that in October, I could only run 4-5 miles at a time. I think that's progress.

***

A couple of weeks later, I went home to Rochester for my spring break, which synced up with one of the culminating moments of marathon training: the elusive 20-mile run. Runners don't need to run the full 26.2 miles in training. 20 miles offers a good indication of whether someone is ready for race day. You're supposed to treat it like a dress rehearsal by practicing what kind of fluids to take, what clothes to wear, etc. I had successfully run

18 miles the week before, and I was ready to take on this next challenge.

I started off by running towards my grandma's house, which was eight miles away. I picked up a Gatorade bottle that I had placed on her front porch, along with a GU Energy Gel. The gels are gooey sugar packets that provide carbs, caffeine, and sugar throughout an endurance event. Although the consistency of the gel was gross, I felt my energy come back after taking it. As I ran on the same long road for about two hours, I listened to music on my iPod to break up the mundane feeling that was settling in.

With five miles to go, I felt a wave of exhaustion wash over me. Even though I had created a playlist with a lot of pop songs with steady beats, no song could provide the necessary revitalization that I needed. It was 16 degrees out, with a biting windchill of 5 degrees. I could not stay warm. I tried to imagine the hot shower that awaited me, as well as the delicious quesadillas my mom was making for dinner. I practically salivated thinking about washing them down with a Blue Moon beer – anything to distract me from the miles that remained. In the end, I finished in 3 hours and 12 minutes (9:21 per mile). Although this was slower than my goal race pace (9:09 per mile) to run under four hours, I hoped that better weather conditions on race day would help improve my pace.

As I walked around my neighborhood for my cooldown, the soreness kicked in. Despite the lasting fatigue, I was proud that I finished my longest run ever. As I sat with my parents and wolfed down my dinner, I told them I was excited about the upcoming taper, when I'd cut back on my mileage to let my body recover before the big day. Being home for spring break during the beginning of the taper allowed me to rest from both the intensity of grad school and marathon training.

***

Even though I was nervous, I was excited for race day and I chatted about the marathon to anyone who listened. On one of my final long runs before the marathon, I struck up a conversation with a fellow runner as we both waited for the stoplight to change. He asked what I was training for, and I eagerly told him about my upcoming marathon debut. When the light turned green, we fell into step together and ran a couple of miles side by side. His final remark stuck with me, as he commented: "No matter what time you finish the race, 4 hours, 5 hours, it doesn't matter, because you will *beat the world!* This is a big deal!"

I knew that the marathon was a physical journey and required a lot of strength training, but it required mental training too. My big mental strategy and way to honor those who I love was to dedicate a mile to them. I wrote their names on my pace band that I planned to wear during the race and wrote each of them a letter to say acknowledge how much they meant to me. I thought I could focus on each loved one for one mile, roughly nine minutes at a time, and the thought of them would inspire me to keep going.

***

The night before the marathon, I went to bed early, filled with anticipation, like a child waiting for Christmas Day to finally arrive. I couldn't wait for that magical morning to come. I managed to fall asleep by 10:15 and did not stir until my alarm went off at 4 a.m. After a light breakfast and some stretching, I took the metro to RFK Stadium, where the race started and ended. The only people on the train at 6 a.m. were other runners. Unlike the normal noise of the metro, the train was filled with hushed, nervous-but-excited chatter.

It was pitch-black and 30 degrees when I arrived. I took off my sweats, checked my bag, and headed to the starting line. I shivered in my long-sleeve top and shorts: I dressed lightly, knowing I would warm up once we got moving. As I approached the corrals, I positioned myself in the 8:30-9:15 per mile section, in the hopes that I could keep up with the other people trying to run the marathon under four hours. In the last moments of silence before the starting gun went off and my new adventure began, I took one last deep breath.

My parents, who had driven in from Rochester to watch

me race, cheered as I crossed the starting line. I tried to settle into a comfortable pace. The first few miles went by quickly, but at mile 7, my right sock rolled under my ankle. I pulled over to the curb to hastily untie my shoe and fix my sock. Concerned about making up the time I lost, I picked up the pace (a rookie mistake). I grinned as I ran by my parents at mile 11. I felt completely present and enjoyed all of these small moments as they occurred throughout the race. I looked down at my pace band, which listed projected times to hit for each mile. Mistakenly, I thought I was 4 minutes behind my goal, and picked up the pace.

When I reached the halfway point (13.1 miles) in 1:52, I realized I misread my pace band, and could break 4 hours with room to spare. I saw my parents again a few miles later and felt strong as I waved at them. The next few miles flew by, especially mile 17, which went downhill. I knew that my friends Wes, Seth, and Mary from grad school were going to be standing at mile 20. I told them to come around 10 a.m., thinking that's how long it would take for me to run 20 miles. Thankfully, they arrived early. I yelled out to them: they were surprised to see me running ahead of schedule. It gave me a laugh and a mental boost.

I was moved by the marathon's symphony of sounds. Spectators cheered, blasted music, clapped, and rang cowbells. Suddenly, we hit a quiet section, where the crowds were sparse, and the silence became deafening. I could hear the swishing of peoples' clothes, the soft thuds of their feet, and even the various kinds of breathing. Some runners breathed with relative control, others I could hear groaning in ways that indicated that they were struggling. One man in particular made a moaning sound with every exhalation. Even though my legs felt tired, I did my best to get away from this heavy breather, as he was a reminder of how hard it was to run the marathon.

At mile 21, the fatigue became all-consuming. *Was this the infamous "wall" I had heard about?* The combination of drinking PowerAde and eating GU left a sickeningly sweet taste in my mouth and my stomach hurt. My legs were turning into lead: it felt like I was going nowhere. I thought about my list of loved ones I had dedicated each mile to: I owed it to each of them to run strong throughout the whole race, even during these harder parts. At mile 23, I told myself there was only a 5k left, and that I would be done with it soon. Then two miles left, but two hills to climb: each felt enormous. Although I felt like I was barely picking up my legs, I passed the 25-mile mark, indicating that I "just" had 1.2 miles to go.

Finally, I passed the 26th mile marker, meaning that 385 meters (slightly less than a lap around a track) was all that remained. I dug in to find that last bit of energy I had stored, and ran as fast as I could to the finish. I could see my friends and parents leaning over the barricade, cheering for me. "Here comes Vanessa Taylor!" The officials announced my name over the loudspeaker as I crossed the finish line with my hands raised in triumph. The feeling of pride that washed over me as I crossed the finish line was unparalleled. Nothing could diminish this moment, and all of my fears of failure were wiped away on this one special day. I had managed to complete the marathon in a time that put me in the top third of the entire field:

Finishing time: 3:52:18 (8:52/mile)

Overall place 743/2,094

I was shocked with my finishing time. In the weeks leading up to the race, I had been filled with many doubts about my goal. In the end, I ended up surpassing even my most ambitious goal of a sub four-hour marathon.

After getting my finisher's medal, I was promptly hugged by my parents and friends. If this was the runner's high, it felt incredible. Although my legs carried me through the marathon, I started to feel sore within a few minutes after finishing. In an effort to not stiffen up, I walked around the RFK stadium parking lot, stretched, and even got a much-appreciated free massage. My friends joked that I waddled like a pregnant woman - a shuffling gait that continued for the next two days. Following a long shower and nap, I went out to dinner with my parents and friends. My parents saw that I had finally established a group of supportive friends in D.C., my friends pressed my parents for embarrassing stories about me as a kid, and we all had a great time eating and drinking in celebration of the marathon.

In recapping the day, I wrote, "It was one of the best days of my life. I am in a fair amount of pain from my hips down, but it is completely worth it. I don't think I could've done it without the support from my family and friends. It was an incredible adventure." I instantly knew I wanted to try running another one. My finishing time opened my eyes up to a loftier goal: The Boston Marathon.

Chapter 3: Qualifying for The Boston Marathon

"Every marathon I ran, I knew I had a faster marathon in me." – Dick Beardsley, 1982 runner-up in the famous "Duel in the Sun" Boston Marathon

To the diehard members of the running community, the Boston Marathon needs no explanation. It is the Holy Grail, the People's Olympics, and the oldest continuously-run marathon. After the first modern Olympics in 1896, Americans sought to recreate the fabled distance event in 1897. The creation of the Boston Marathon ushered in the beginning of a new era in distance running. Boston attracts Olympians and world record-holders, but it is also competitive among the masses because of its unique qualifying standard.

Like students who get into Ivy League schools based on their nearly-perfect SAT scores, marathon runners must submit their fastest marathon times to be accepted into Boston. Only the top 10% of runners in each age group are admitted to the race. Securing that precious BQ (Boston Qualifier) is the running equivalent of earning a Ph.D. Both are difficult to do, many who try fail to do so, but both are widely recognized as a special distinction in their respective fields.

When I ran my first marathon in 2009, the qualifying standard for women my age (18-34) was 3:40:59. That was 12 minutes away from what I ran in my first marathon (3:52:18) – about 30 seconds per mile. While my debut marathon was largely successful, I also knew I made some mistakes that could be corrected in the future.

A month after my debut marathon, I watched the Boston Marathon on TV. Inspired by the Americans (Kara Goucher and Ryan Hall) who placed third in their races, I was full of desire to participate in that hallowed race. Later that day, I wrote in my blog,

It is my intention to be in the 2010 Boston Marathon. I need to slice off 12 minutes from my time. A lot of work will need to be done between now and then. There are the elite runners who go to Boston to try to win, but for most runners, it's the ability to get to the starting line that counts. This is the Olympics for the regular marathoner, and I want to be there.

***

My athletic training became the perfect complement to my academic training. Setting my sights on qualifying for Boston helped me to find my focus in grad school.

Towards the end of the Spring 2009 semester, I met with Dr. Sherman, a professor of early modern history, to discuss my progress on a final paper. She asked how the end of the semester was wrapping up. As I wearily told her about the other papers and difficult exams ahead, Dr. Sherman interjected: "You just ran a marathon! This shouldn't be as hard." I countered, "But the marathon was fun!" She was surprised that I found running easier than a Latin exam. Latin continued to be a struggle for me, and repeatedly made me question if I would be able to complete the coursework required to advance to the doctoral program.

My Latin class culminated in a morphology exam, which tested our knowledge about the formulations and structures of words. In order to pass the class, students had to earn a 90 or higher on the exam. However, the test was so notoriously hard to pass that we were given six attempts to take the difficult exam.

Veterans of the class told me to sit for the exam for the first time in January to get a sense of how I'd do. I prepped all week, knowing that I wouldn't likely pass on the first try, but that I should shoot for a 70 on this attempt. I opened the envelope, and like a house of cards in the face of a gust of wind, all of the verb charts I had in my head quickly crumbled. The remaining hour was spent picking up the remaining fragments of what I could remember.

The following class, Professor Patel slid my exam face down on my desk. *55.* I barely knew half of the material. I had five chances left to pass the class.

My friends, including Wes, fared better, ultimately passing on the third try. They had clinched their victory, while I was breathlessly trying to catch up. While they high-fived each other and invited me to celebrate with them over drinks, I sipped my beer and started to think about my goal for the next time. I hoped to make incremental strides, but even though my score improved 15 points between attempts 1-3, I regressed in the fourth attempt. Each time I sat for the exam, I felt like Charlie Brown running towards Lucy holding the football, expecting each time not to fall down. Each time I got the exam back, I felt flattened. Despite the hours I spent each day pouring over my flashcards, my efforts felt futile.

If I failed this class, it would signal to everyone – my professors, my classmates, and my family, that I wasn't ready to become a medieval historian, and that the school had made a mistake in admitting me. That fear drove me to study even harder. I became more anxious as the end of the semester approached. On the sixth and final try, walking up the three flights of marble stairs to the Latin department felt like I was walking to my own academic execution.

I passed the exam by a single point. While I celebrated this achievement, I still worried about my proficiency in the language. My overall grade in the class was a B-. That was low compared to my classmates, who all earned As. I dreaded the advanced Latin classes that awaited me the following year. But with the arrival of summer, I was looking forward to a break where I could catch up on some fun reading.

***

I've been an avid reader my entire life. My love for reading was one of the reasons why studying history was perfectly suited to my interests. Growing up, I used to sneak books at the dinner table. Even if it was to drive across town to visit my grandparents, I packed multiple books in the car to accompany me on the journey. I could never get enough reading time.

In third grade, my teacher came up with a reading challenge for our class, complete with a chart on the chalkboard to keep track of how many books we read. When I completed the chart (100 books) at Thanksgiving break, Mrs. DeMarte started to keep track of my books separately. By the end of the year, I had read 437 books, and as a congratulatory gift for being the top reader, she presented me with a leatherbound illustrated edition of Louisa May Alcott's *Little Women*. "May you never stop loving to read," she said as she gave me a hug on the last day of class. My ongoing love of books was one of the main reasons I was excited about grad school.

With the intensity of coursework, any pleasure reading could not happen until the semester was over. My parents had recently given me a new running memoir by a woman named Kathrine Switzer called *Marathon Woman: Running the Race to Revolutionize Women's Sports*. The book patiently sat on the shelf until May. Once I picked it up, I was completely hooked as I learned about the obstacles women faced in the fight for equality in athletics.

In 1898, a doctor in the German Journal of Physical Education advised women against exercise because "violent movements of the body can cause a shift in the position and a loosening of the uterus as well as prolapse and bleeding, with resulting sterility, thus defeating a woman's true purpose in life, i.e., the bringing forth of strong children." Female exertion was regarded as unfeminine and dangerous. There was even a three-dribble rule in women's basketball designed to prevent a prolapsed uterus.

Additionally, women were not allowed to compete in long-distance running events. The 800 meters event (2 laps around the track) was banned from the Olympics after 1928 when, on a hot day, the women pushed themselves to exhaustion – as you do in a short-distance event. The organizers were horrified by this display of exertion from the "gentler sex," and recommended that the event be banned in future Olympics. It was not until 1960 that the event was reinstated.

Women who exercised were told that they wouldn't be able to bear children, they'd grow a mustache, and they'd never be able to attract a husband. It was not until 1972, when Title IX was ratified, that women were given equal athletic opportunities as men. Incidentally, this was the same year that the Boston Marathon finally allowed women to participate in their race.

Although the Boston Marathon was a men's-only race, in 1966, a young woman named Bobbi Gibb hid in the bushes near the start line and joined the race, becoming the first unofficial female finisher. A year later, in 1967, Kathrine Switzer, a journalism major at Syracuse University made history when she registered for the race as "K.V. Switzer." Donning bulky sweats, she blended in with the men on a snowy day. She was excited to participate in this historic race, and began the marathon without a hitch.

However, word started to spread that there was "a girl" in the race, which inflamed Jock Semple, one of the race officials. 2 miles into the race, Kathrine heard footsteps beside her, but not those of her fellow competitors, but of Jock Semple. He lunged at her and yelled, "Get the hell out of my race, and give me those numbers!" Jock tried to rip off her race bib, and lunging toward her, pushed Kathrine. Although she stumbled, she managed to stay upright. Suddenly, wham! Her boyfriend Tom, an all-American hammer thrower, shoved Jock aside, causing the old official to fall to the ground. The photographers on the press truck, who had been eager to document a woman running the marathon, captured the confrontation in a series of three distinct frames. Afraid of what could happen next, Kathrine surged forward, continuing on her way to finish the race.

After a scary episode like that, I could not imagine running 24 more miles with fear and adrenaline coursing through me. Yet, Kathrine was determined to finish, "on my hands and my knees, if I have to," she later recalled. She knew that if she failed to complete the race, it would set women's athletics back and prove to all the naysayers that women were incapable of running long distances. Kathrine pressed on, and finished the marathon. The photographs documenting her attack instantly became an iconic moment in the history of the Boston Marathon.

I loved *Marathon Woman* because it was filled with colorful examples of a woman who continued to persist in the face of adversity. Kathrine faced many naysayers: both people who believed that women lacked the endurance to compete in long-distance events, and from authorities who sought to prevent the inclusion of women's athletics. Her willingness to work hard, even amid such a sexist environment, was inspiring. Kathrine's story of tenacity was what I needed to keep in my head while I struggled to find my footing in graduate school.

***

The summer ended, and it was back to school for the second year of my master's program. I was excited about my classes, especially a class that Dr. Jansen was teaching on late medieval hagiography (writing about the lives of saints). Although I grew up attending Sunday school, my knowledge about medieval saints was limited. I found it fascinating to read canonization records: legal records that were assembled in order to establish a person's sanctity. I loved learning about miracle stories where saints intervened to save supplicants from the plague, sinking ships, and other bizarre and wondrous episodes.

During this semester, I also needed to start considering what my options were for pursuing a Ph.D. I thought it was in my best interest to stay at CUA for my doctorate, as I already had started to make meaningful connections with my professors. But the big factor that determined whether or not I could stay at CUA had to do with money. I had earned a partial scholarship during my master's degree. However, if I was going to commit to a doctoral program, I needed full funding. I already had accumulated about $50,000 in student debt from both my B.A. and my M.A. I could not in good conscience take on any more loans. The most promising path was a TA fellowship, which would cover tuition and come with a modest stipend. To secure a fellowship, I needed to connect with our new department chair.

Our outgoing chair, Dr. Riley, the one who saw me smack my head into the door on my first day, had retired in May. I had never formally met Dr. Muller, our new chair. Nearly trembling, I sat in his office that October as I told him about my first year at CUA. Trying to project poise and confidence, I stated that I wanted to stay on for the Ph.D. program, and was interested in applying for a TA position. After I gave my opening pitch, Dr. Muller sat back in his seat, thought pensively for a moment, and then proceeded to express his hesitancy about the department's ability to fund me in the doctoral program,

"You know, Vanessa, a doctoral program is not easy. There are many rigorous steps, and not everyone makes it through. Moreover, earning a Ph.D. doesn't guarantee that you'll get a job in academia. Are you prepared to deal with that disappointment? These are some of the things you'll have to consider when making the decision about whether to pursue your doctorate..."

My heart sank as he continued to talk. Dr. Muller said that my professors needed to vouch for me in order for him to consider giving me a fellowship. Still, he noted that even positive references did not guarantee I'd be awarded a position. My future at Catholic felt uncertain. I pulled myself together to make it through the rest of the meeting without my eyes watering, and then he escorted me out.

Once I left O'Connell Hall, a few tears trickled down my face, as a million questions swirled around in my head. What did my future hold if I didn't go into academia? I loved medieval history, and I couldn't imagine the next phase of my life without school. There was no plan B. I didn't know what to do. I felt dejected. It was hard to not feel like a fraud. Whether it was a lecture or even a department happy hour, I felt that I had to perform well by asking some sort of interesting question or helping advance the discussion. If my contribution to the conversation seemed sub-par, I believed that it added a tally mark to the column for reasons why the department shouldn't accept me as a doctoral student. In my classes, I imagined that any paper grade below an "A" caused me to be moved to the "no" column. I worried that because I received extensive criticism on papers during my master's degree, how would I ever make it through the grueling process of writing a book-length dissertation?

There were never any concrete moments that clearly pointed to failure that semester. I didn't bomb a presentation, fail a paper, or say anything completely idiotic in discussion. Even though I often saw my classmates skimming the assigned books at the last minute, I carefully prepared for class. I'd come to my seminars with a list of detailed notes and talking points in an effort to make a positive impression on my professors. Despite doing all of the reading, I often left discussion feeling defeated. My professors never said my statements were invalid. Yet, the rather flat responses they gave to my contributions, compared to the more receptive feedback they gave to some of my classmates, signaled to me that I gave an underwhelming performance.

I did not know that "imposter syndrome" is a common feeling among graduate students. American psychologists Pauline Clance and Suzanne Imes coined this term in 1978, describing it as a feeling of "phoniness in people who believe that they are not intelligent, capable or creative despite evidence of high achievement." In class, I feared that the mask would be ripped off, and that my professors would realize that it was a mistake for me to be there – that I did not belong there. I didn't realize that other grad students also shared that feeling. I wish I knew then that the criticism that my professors gave me was meant to groom me for excellence, not to discourage me. These comments weren't personal judgments – my professors were trying to help me become a better writer. Although it's hard to not take writing feedback personally, I've also subsequently looked back at some of those early papers. They weren't great and certainly benefited from candid assessment.

***

Amid my academic uncertainty, I sought to gain some control over my personal life. I finally broke up with Matthew on the phone, reading nearly verbatim a statement I had reworked all summer on a notepad. I was afraid of losing my focus, or that I'd get interrupted, that I wanted all the thoughts that had been rattling around in my head spelled out precisely. I figured that we'd never speak again. This was my last chance to release what I had kept bottled inside for years. I told him that he didn't support me or respect me, and that his behavior was not "caring," as he tried to argue, but controlling. When he said, "I'll never forgive you," I knew it was over. I was finally free.

While it was something I should've done years before, the fallout was still upsetting. A part of me was grieving the end of my first significant relationship, but what I was really mourning was all of the time I wasted with him. It wasn't as if there was someone waiting in the wings, but there were things I missed out on during college because of him. I blew off friends to spend time with him, and I defended him against anyone, including my family, who dared to suggest I could do better. I had jeopardized many meaningful relationships for him, and all of those bad memories haunted me. In those five years together, I lost so much of myself - it took a long time to find those parts of me again.

The breakup changed what I expected in a romantic relationship. Although I wasn't interested in dating again in the immediate aftermath, I vowed that I would no longer settle. Instead, I told myself I would demand the respect and support that I knew I truly deserved.

Despite all of this tumult, I was laser-focused on the Marine Corps Marathon. I was determined to throw all of my energy into qualifying for Boston. It was a hot fall in D.C. I sweated it out through my 20-mile runs, even doing one 22-mile run when I ran through the sprinklers on the National Mall in an effort to cool down on a 91-degree day. It was hot, it was hard, and my ability to perform in adverse conditions made me optimistic about race day.

***

Going into my second marathon, I also acquired a secret weapon that ultimately transformed my running. Sarah Spalding was a fellow graduate student who was light-years ahead of me, both in running and in school. As an undergrad, she ran for Duke and when she moved to D.C., Sarah ran for one of the local elite teams and had teammates who had qualified for the Olympic Trials. Sarah had entered the doctoral program at CUA when I began my master's, and was moving quickly through her coursework. After I had finished my first marathon, she commented one day after class that there was a real possibility that I could qualify for Boston. Her remark legitimized the glimmer of hope I had been carrying with me for months.

After sitting together for a lecture on heretical movements in early Christianity, Sarah asked how my training was going. To my surprise, she offered to help pace me for the marathon, similar to the elite runners who had their own assigned pacers to help them maintain an even cadence when seeking to break a particular time barrier. Sarah said that she could jump into the race at mile 16, and run the last 10 miles with me to keep me on pace to break 3:40. I was flattered that someone who I admired both academically and athletically took an interest in helping me. All I had to do was keep a steady pace for 16 miles, and then I could mentally hitch my wagon to Sarah and hang on for the last 10 miles.

Two days before the marathon, I went to the race expo to pick up my racing chip, t-shirt, and bib number. The most enjoyable part of the expo was that I got to meet and speak to Kathrine Switzer, author of *Marathon Woman*. When she signed my copy of her book, she wrote "Here's to a BQ...no matter what, it's a victory already and the results are magic. Go for it!" She asked me if I understood what that meant, that training for something significant is a victory in itself, and the results manifest themselves in many parts of life. I hoped that I would meet her again, as she provided genuine motivation and inspiration.

***

On October 25, 2009, I woke up two minutes before my alarm went off at 4 a.m. I took my ability to wake up naturally to be a good sign. I listened to pump-up music on my iPod as I walked from the metro to the Runners Village near the Pentagon. The song that ultimately captured the months of hard work leading up to race day was "All These Things I've Done" by The Killers. I listened to it as I walked into the Runners Village, thinking about all the things I had done that had culminated in this special moment. I had broken up with Matthew and was done accepting unacceptable behavior. I was chasing bigger things in every aspect of my life and this was a day to celebrate that.

Over the summer, I had discovered an online Marine Corps Marathon forum, where people logged in daily to post their workouts, comment on other peoples' posts, and offer little doses of motivation. Because only about a dozen people posted regularly, we quickly got to know each other in this virtual environment. They knew how school was going, that I broke up with Matthew, and that I was hoping to qualify for Boston. It was exciting to finally meet after months of writing to each other. We hugged like old friends. The community bond became strong enough that in the ensuing years, two of the forum members alternated hosting a running forum meet-up the night before the race. We all cherish the one time each year that we all get to be together "in real life."

All morning, the announcers over the loudspeakers said that we had the best weather in race history (50 degrees, sunny, with little to no wind) and I believed it. It was a gorgeous day. Promptly at 8 a.m., the starting cannon (they used all of the military pomp for this race and even had a military flyover before the race) went off. Boston or bust – it was time to run!

With over 20,000 people in the race, the first few miles were a few seconds slower than marathon pace. By mile 4, the crowds had thinned out and I was hitting my stride and on pace. The hills were not bad, especially because I had practiced on routes that had steeper elevation. Every block was filled with bands and lots of cheering. The spectators' signs made me laugh, such as "You think you're tired - my arms are killing me," "Kick some asphalt," and one held up by someone dressed as Obi-Wan Kenobi, "May the course be with you."

Wearing a bright pink top at mile 10, Sarah leaned over the barrier separating the spectators from the runners and yelled out, "Go Vanessa! I'll see you at mile 16!" That was good motivation for me. I told myself, "3 miles to the halfway point, and then 3 miles to Sarah after that." I hit the halfway point around 1:49, which meant I was right on pace to finish in 3:40. But, the next few miles went by slowly, and I started to feel tired. My watch couldn't lie: my pace slowed down and my Boston qualifying time was slipping away.

Having Sarah jump in at mile 16 was a breath of fresh air. Sarah held my Gatorade bottle for me, and said, "Don't talk. I'll do all the talking for the next 10 miles." At one point, she even yelled for people to cheer for me, which gave me a boost. Throughout the race, Sarah kept repeating, "You're looking strong," "You look relaxed," and "You're handling this very well," as she handed me my Gatorade whenever I needed a drink. She also picked out certain runners and instructed me to focus on passing them. This tactic was important, because I needed to make up some time in order to achieve my goal of qualifying for Boston.

I hadn't set any other goal for the race and was petrified that I would miss the qualifying time (3:40:59) by a few crushing seconds. Sarah also knew I was slightly behind but devised a plan to help me make up for lost time (which is difficult to do late in the race). Sarah kept an eye on her watch, so that I could focus on keeping up with the steady pace. We ran around the National Mall, and after that Sarah told me, "We're leaving D.C. for good now." Soldiering on, we crossed an enormous bridge at mile 20, which featured someone dressed as the devil holding an ominous sign that read "The end is near." At this point, Sarah was encouraging me to hang in there: "Now, you can use all of those speed workouts that you've been doing to pick up the pace and pick off others." Although I didn't feel that I was accelerating, I managed to pass a few people. We arrived at Crystal City, which had lots of music and spectators, which were welcome distractions to the fatigue and pain that were starting to settle in. Then she said, "Only a 5k left."

A 5k (3.1 miles) by itself goes by fast. But not after 23 miles. Sarah kept repeating all of her mantras, and added, "You're going to get your qualifying time and you are going to smash your PR." She instructed me to stop looking at my watch. As a distant roar became louder, Sarah asked, "Can you hear that? That's the finish. You are almost there." Because she wasn't an official race participant, Sarah stepped off of the course at the 26-mile marker, and yelled, "Go!" The final stretch of the course runs up a steep hill, past the famous Iwo Jima Memorial. We were flanked by a set of Marines cheering us on as we sought to vanquish this final challenge. I dug in, found the last bit of strength I had, and charged up the hill towards the finish arch.

I pushed and pushed and as I crossed the finish line, I saw that the race clock still said "3:39." I got my BQ! Pure joy set in at that point. Despite slowing down in the middle of the race, I managed to qualify for one of the most prestigious marathons in the world. I couldn't stop smiling. A Marine gave me my finisher's medal and offered hearty congratulations. I found Sarah, and we hugged and cheered for joy. Sarah really made a difference in helping me get back on pace and qualify for Boston. The official results were posted when I got back:

Finishing time: 3:39:55 (8:23/mile)

Overall place: 2,061/20,936

For the next few days, it was painful to walk. I even winced visibly as I stepped off the curb walking to class. A passerby looked at me inquisitively, wondering why my face looked pained while performing a seemingly-simple action. I yelled, "I ran a marathon yesterday - my quads are killing me!" He laughed. Despite the soreness, I was ecstatic. Sarah encouraged me to "bask in my Boston glory," which captured my mood for weeks to come. But the immediate Boston glory quickly gave way to something else – the desire to train for and successfully compete at the greatest amateur running stage in the world – the 2010 Boston Marathon.

Chapter 4: The Boston Marathon

"When I go to the Boston Marathon now, I have wet shoulders—women fall into my arms crying. They're weeping for joy because running has changed their lives.

They feel they can do anything." – Kathrine Switzer, 1st official female finisher of the Boston Marathon in 1967

November 10, 2009
Dear Vanessa,
This is to notify you that your entry into the 114th Boston Marathon on Monday, April 19, 2010 has been accepted. We look forward to seeing you in April! Best of luck in your training!
Sincerely,
Boston Athletic Association

Getting the official letter made the dream of getting into Boston a reality. The acceptance letter reminded me a lot of how I felt when I got into Holy Cross. Both represented goals I had worked towards for a long time. There is something incredibly special about the Boston Marathon: its storied history, the qualifying time, the competition, or the quest to set foot upon sacred ground, that brings runners from all 50 states, and nearly 100 countries together for one day. I couldn't wait to be a part of it.

***

A few weeks after the Marine Corps Marathon, Sarah offered to design my training schedule in the build-up to Boston. People pay good money to hire a private coach, and here was someone who volunteered to do it for free. Sarah's plan was a clear shift from my mundane training schedule from my first two marathons, and instead, offered a concerted plan to sharpen my speed and make me a stronger, faster runner.

Once a month for the next four months, Sarah emailed me a detailed training plan for each four-week cycle. These training plans always appeared daunting at first. In the first month of training for Boston, I'd cover about 200 miles, some on hills, some on the track, some slow, some fast. Here's a sample of what one of my first training weeks for Boston 2010 looked like:

Monday, January 4: OFF
Tuesday, January 5: 2.5-mile warm-up; 6 x 1-mile repeats, aiming to get faster with each interval. Jog 1 lap between each rep and aim for 7:45, 7:40, 7:35, 7:30, 7:25, 7:20. 2.5-mile cooldown. Total mileage: 12.5 miles
Wednesday, January 6: 6 miles easy
Thursday, January 7: 8 miles easy
Friday, January 8: OFF
Saturday, January 9: 14 miles easy
Sunday, January 10: 7 miles easy
Total Mileage: 47.5 miles

For comparison, this early week of Boston training was equal to my highest mileage week in the buildup to the Marine Corps Marathon. Now, I was running with greater intensity, and there were still three months until the Boston Marathon. Amid the high mileage, I had two non-running days built into the schedule, which either were off completely or intended for some sort of cross-training. Moreover, every fourth week in the cycle was a "cut back week," which was about 25% lighter than the previous three weeks and designed to give me time to recover. The idea is to run your hard days hard, and easy days easy. The body responds to different efforts better than a consistent pace day-in, day-out, and while you may feel "good" on an easy day, respecting the effort level is an important part of becoming a stronger, smarter runner.

Sarah served as a double role model. She was the fastest person I knew, and was making great strides through her graduate program. It gave me a lot to aspire to, and Sarah seemed to demonstrate that a hard-working ethic on the road could translate into success in school.

***

At the beginning of the Spring 2010 semester, I prepared for another semester of intensive Latin. I was fortunate enough to have friends in the course with me, as well as classmates who were veterans of the class and could offer helpful Latin advice. My friends, knowing how nervous I was about the semester, reminded me, "If you can qualify for Boston, you can surely do Latin!" Unlike my newly-found confidence in running, I felt wholly inadequate in a field that was central to my professional career.

It was my final semester of required Latin: medieval Latin. I had naively hoped that because the translation assignments were more tied to the content discussed in my history classes, the assignments would become easier to complete. Wrong. Medieval Latin was more advanced and the shaky grasp of the language I had felt all the more fragile. My middling test scores caused me to fear that Latin could jeopardize my acceptance into the doctoral program.

I was spending a disproportionate amount of time on Latin: both in comparison to my friends, who finished their homework in an hour or two, and compared to the time I put into my other classes. Even after our group study sessions finished, I migrated to the library until it closed, trying to furiously prepare for the next day's class. Although I should've slept soundly from the combined exertion of marathon training and studying, I'd wake up in the middle of the night for hours on end, worrying about Latin. Each morning, I felt exhausted and miserable, wondering yet again if my love of medieval history was worth this constant struggle.

One day, when it was my turn to translate a passage from St. Augustine's *Confessions*, I tried to clumsily work my way through what ultimately translated as,

"For if there are times past and future, I wish to know where they are... Wherever they are and whatever they are they exist only as present. Although we tell of past things as true, they are drawn out of the memory, not the things themselves, which have already passed, but words constructed from the images of the perceptions which were formed in the mind."

If that seems confusing in English, it seemed even more jumbled in Latin. I kept stumbling, like a runner trying to reach the finish line but collapsing, rising, only to fall again. My new professor, Professor Barnett, put me out of my misery by calling on someone else to translate the rest of the passage.

I had put all of my energy studying for our midterm. However, as soon as I opened the exam, I knew I was in for a doozy. A few days later, Professor Barnett handed back the exams. Mine didn't have a grade on it, only "See me after class" in red letters. My heart sunk. I had sealed my fate as a failed medievalist. Sitting through the rest of the class was painful. My eyes kept brimming with tears and I felt like I needed to throw up. I packed up my books, and timidly followed him to his office. Perched in his wingback chair, Professor Barnett lowered his glasses and sighed,

"Vanessa, you seem to really be struggling in the class. I know you're putting in the work, but it's clear that not everything is clicking in the way it should be at this point. I want you to consider auditing the class instead of taking it for a grade. I think there's a lot you can gain from the class, but I don't want to see you fail. Maybe if the pressure is off from getting a grade, you'll be able to make more progress. Talk to Dr. Jansen to see if she'd be on board with this."

I thanked him, and walked out with my head down. I emailed Dr. Jansen, who was in Europe on sabbatical, and explained what Professor Barnett recommended. She immediately approved of me auditing the class, which offered a sense of temporary relief. I wasn't going to wash out of the program. While this wasn't a blemish on my transcript, I felt ashamed about my ineptitude with Latin. In my head, it was another tick to add to the "bad graduate student" tally that I couldn't seem to get out of my head.

***

The 2010 winter was a rough one for Washington. I was accustomed to long, tough winters with lots of snow growing up in Rochester, NY and then experienced similarly harsh weather while attending college in Massachusetts. My first winter in D.C. taught me that the entire city tended to fall apart when there was even an inch or two of snow. Yet, in February 2010, we got walloped with back-to-back storms, which the meteorologists referred to as "Snowmaggedon" and "Snowpocalypse." In the first storm, we got 2 feet of snow, and before the city could recover, we were hit with a second storm 48 hours later.

The roads were terrible for weeks and were not ideal for marathon training. I couldn't stand the thought of slogging my runs out on the boring treadmill. However, there was a mile stretch on the perimeter of campus that was fully plowed and more importantly, had no black ice. Until the conditions of the roads improved, I completed all of my runs on this clear one-mile path. Back and forth I ran, much to the amusement of the campus safety officer who always sat in a car parked by the entrance of campus. When I had to run 12 miles, I counted the "laps" in my head (this was before I had a GPS watch), slowly accruing the mileage as I ran up and down the stretch again and again. These were solitary runs on cold winter mornings. On days that I had speed workouts, I mapped out the quarter-mile breakdowns and brought a stopwatch to time myself. Although it wasn't a perfect solution, this clear path ensured I maintained my endurance, until enough snow melted and I happily returned to my regular routes.

When I needed a break from my history books, I researched the Boston Marathon. I wanted to learn more about the course and the storied history of the race that had captured the imagination of millions of runners. Whenever I heard the word "Boston," butterflies fluttered in my stomach, as I felt a surge of excitement.

But not all aspects of the preparation were enjoyable. In those more difficult moments, I had to remind myself of the prize I was chasing. One day, I was at the student fitness center to do some strength work. As I did a set of planks, my arms started to shake as the seconds ticked off. I recited to myself, "Boston, Boston." During the end of long runs, as I started to tire, I'd visualize the Boston Marathon, as an attempt to remain focused and to stay strong through the end of the run. I had read about the power of positive thinking and learned that many elite marathoners use some sort of mantra or power word during tough moments. I decided that "Boston" would be my power word. Any time I felt apprehensive about the race or a history paper, I'd think "Boston, Boston," and used that excitement to banish my worries. I also had a power song that got me excited for the race. Any time I heard "I Gotta Feeling," by The Black Eyed Peas, which had been popular all year, I felt in the groove and ready to tackle the day's challenges.

***

In an effort to connect with the D.C. running community, I participated in the Saturday group runs organized by Pacers – a local running store. Eager to have some company for my weekend 20-mile run, I showed up to the store at 8 a.m. As the other runners started to assemble and chat about their upcoming races, I realized that I was out of my league. Peter, who was tall and skinny, loomed over me as he told me about his goal to break three hours at Boston. Annie, the only other woman there, had a 3:10 PR that made her as fast as the guys. I was going to be the slowest one there, and I told them I feared that I'd hold the group back. "Nonsense!" they assured me, "We run our long runs at a conversational pace. We'll make sure it feels comfortable for you."

We took off, and what was an easy pace for them was fast for me. Peter, who was the designated group leader, noticed that I had grown quiet and sidled up next to me around mile 12. "Are you okay, Vanessa?" he inquired. "Yeah," I grunted. "I'm trying to not slow you guys down."

Peter took it upon himself to encourage me to keep going. He entertained me with stories about running Chicago, New York, and his own debut at the Boston Marathon. His movements were fluid and effortless as he carried the weight of the conversation and pacing duties. I did my best to chime in with open-ended questions that he could talk about for miles. Peter's anecdotes kept me distracted as we wound our way through Rock Creek Park. We finished the run in 2 hours and 54 minutes – the fastest 20-mile run I had ever done in practice. And I was exhausted.

I finished feeling concerned about my ability to perform well in Boston. If I felt tired in training, how was I going to run Boston successfully when I wanted to do it at a faster pace on a harder course?

After reflecting on my training on the ride home, I had to remind myself of the reasons why this was a successful run. Peter and Annie had been running marathons for years: I was still a relatively new runner. Additionally, it was completely normal to be tired at the end of running 20 miles. I had completed a difficult track workout a few days prior and was in the middle of high-volume training. Finally, I needed to celebrate that this was my fastest 20-mile time ever.

So why was I hard on myself? Was it because it felt tough to push through those final miles? Or was it because the imposter syndrome that had become ingrained in my academic life had also encroached on my running world as well? It seemed to be the latter: the insecurities I felt permeated many aspects of my life.

***

That spring, I had one eye on Boston and another on trying to secure enough funding so I could continue onto the doctoral program. Following Dr. Muller's suggestion, I met with each of my professors to let them know that I was interested in becoming a TA, and that their recommendation would go a long way. One by one, each professor offered their endorsement but also encouraged me to look for funding elsewhere.

My hopes were raised when I was named a semifinalist for the Lilly Graduate Fellows Program: a competitive national fellowship. Not only would the three-year stipend cover my tuition, but I'd also meet annually with an engaging cohort that shared my academic interests. I couldn't imagine a more engaging academic experience that would be both financially rewarding and personally fulfilling. My department even set up a practice interview to help me workshop potential answers and arrive at the interview as polished as possible.

Although the two-day interview process was exhausting, I enjoyed the conversations I had with my potential cohort, faculty mentors, and the interview committee. I was confident that I had nailed the answers that I had rehearsed for weeks. Of the 24 semifinalists, 16 would be selected for the fellowship - pretty good odds. As the plane prepared for takeoff to head back to D.C., I relaxed in my seat, feeling confident about Boston and my financial security for the following year. When I returned to campus the next day, I excitedly told all of my professors all about the interview, and that I'd hear back from the committee in a few days.

Later that week, I went to the library to work on one of my final papers. Before getting into my research, I logged into my email,

The Selection Committee has met and made decisions regarding the third cohort of the Lilly Graduate Fellows Program. These decisions were very, very difficult, and we regret that we could not grant fellowships to all of the finalists. Vanessa, we are sorry to inform you that you have not been selected to participate. We wish you only the best as you pursue your academic and professional goals at Catholic University.

I was crushed. My financial security and ability to continue with my studies were once again in jeopardy. It was humiliating to tell my professors that despite my initial confidence, I hadn't landed the fellowship. It was a week before Boston, and while everyone told me to be excited about the race, I still wallowed in my rejection. Yes, I was about to embark on this great adventure of the Boston Marathon, but as soon as the race was over, I'd once again have to face the reality of an unknown future. In a few months, I'd need to reevaluate whether or not I should try to continue onto the Ph.D. It wasn't worth accruing extra debt in the hopes of one day earning my doctorate. While I didn't share these thoughts with my professors, I started to wonder if I'd be better off cutting my losses and leaving academia.

***

On my flight to Boston, I tried to set aside these financial concerns and focus on the race ahead. In order to revive my enthusiasm about the marathon, I looked back at some of my old journal entries from when I first got into running. I was struck with what I wrote after watching the Boston Marathon just one year before,

"It is my intention to be in the 2010 Boston Marathon. This is the Olympics for the regular marathoner, and I want to be there."

Reading it again gave me chills. It wasn't as if I had made a long-shot prediction. I saw a challenging, yet achievable dream, and managed to earn my place at one of the greatest races in the world. I couldn't wait to toe the starting line in Hopkinton.

***

When I got off the plane at Logan Airport, there were Boston Marathon banners everywhere, even at baggage claim. Boston loves this race and the city rolls the red carpet out for its marathoners. The excitement in the air vibrated with an electricity I had never experienced before. The day before the race, I did an easy three-mile jog around Cambridge. I caught a glimpse of the famous Citgo sign (which means 1 mile to go), and harnessed that flash of excitement for the race.

On Marathon Morning, we headed to the bus-loading area: the easiest way to get 25,000 runners from Boston to the start of the race in the small town of Hopkinton. My parents, who drove in from Rochester, were there to put me on the big yellow school bus, which reminded me of the first day of kindergarten. Like they did when I was five years old, they gave me a hug and told me I'd do great, and then it was time to board. I nervously chatted with my seatmate, Terrie, who was also running it for the first time. Talking to her made the long drive go by, and we ended up exchanging addresses and still keep in touch today.

There's something special about the marathon comradery that builds an instantaneous bond between runners.

At the Athletes' Village (Hopkinton High School), thousands of marathoners milled around, trying to pass the time until we were called to the start line. As we moved *en masse* to begin our marathon journey, "I've Got a Feeling," my power song of the season, blared over the loudspeaker. I was already excited, and the music amped me up even more.

All marathon spectators are wonderful: regardless if they know someone running, they come out in droves, offering encouragement and inspiration to the runners. The Boston Marathon spectators are on another level of fandom: half a million spectators line the entire course. They set up mini-water stations on their front lawns and cheer all day. I ran past a group of children who bounced on trampolines while they gave out high-fives to the runners, offering a much-needed chuckle. After my hands became sticky from grabbing cups of Gatorade, I was grateful to the family who handed out wet paper towels, allowing me to clean my hands. The generosity of the human spirit was out in full force.

I tried to maintain a steady pace in the first half of the marathon. The first few miles of the race are downhill, and many runners have often paid the price later on if they've sped down the hills too fast. I thought that if I focused on taking in the spectators and sights, the first few miles would pass by quickly, leaving me enough energy to tackle the hills later on.

The Boston Marathon spans eight towns and cities: each has its own storied history associated with the marathon. As I ran from Ashland, to Framingham, and then to Natick, each town brought a new wave of excitement. I was eager to make my way toward the fabled "Scream Tunnel" in Wellesley, one of the great landmarks of the race.

At mile 12, the women of Wellesley College show up in full force to cheer, give kisses, and offer a boost as runners approach the halfway point. I heard them from afar, and as I approached, their screams reached a fever pitch. They stood on both sides of the road, yelling words of encouragement that seemed to make each step easier. Before I knew it, their cheers once again echoed in the distance. My mind drifted for the next few miles as the crowds thinned out and the loudest sounds became the grunts and heavy breathing of the other runners. As if everything came back into focus, I had arrived at mile 17 – another defining moment of the course.

Unlike most marathon courses, which loop back to the start, Boston is a point-to-point course. There are only five turns in the entire race, and the course is completely straight until mile 17. Once you make that first turn, the Newton Hills are in store, culminating with the infamous Heartbreak Hill (between miles 20 and 21). Heartbreak Hill is the most famous climb in marathon running. In 1936, defending champion John A. "Johnny" Kelley patted Ellison "Tarzan" Brown on the shoulder as he whizzed by him. This patronizing gesture reenergized Brown, who managed to regroup and surge ahead of Kelley, as he raced on to victory, thus breaking Kelley's heart.

I did extensive hill training in D.C. to prepare for these hills. I climbed the first Newton hill and regrouped. "Okay, that wasn't too bad," I thought to myself. I approached the second hill with confidence, and then mentally readied myself to ascend Heartbreak Hill. There were scores of people cheering as we ran up this final summit. Suddenly, I was at the top and made it to Boston College. By this point, it was early in the afternoon, and the college students had been drinking for hours. Although the strong smell of beer didn't sit well with me, the enthusiastic cheering was what I needed as I tried to rally for the final six miles of the race.

I found coming down Heartbreak Hill to be harder than going up it – my quads felt completely trashed. Essentially, when you're descending a hill, your quads are "braking," which hurts more than climbing hills. Thankfully, the Boston College students continued to cheer loudly and that helped to pull me along. 5 miles to go. I tried to break down the remainder of the race in one-mile increments. 4 miles left, then 3 miles, then 2. I reached Brookline – the final town before Boston. The intensity of the crowd picked up. I knew I could finish, but every step felt hard. The Citgo sign loomed in the distance. I put my head down and ignored it – it was like a mirage and made Boston seem closer than it was in reality.

People were walking and even staggering at mile 25. I tried to run tall and confident, even though my energy was flagging. With one turn remaining, I kept looking for the sign pointing to Boylston Street. The crowds were screaming as I got closer. My moment of victory was almost here.

Finally, I made the famous turn – 385 yards to go. I could see the beautiful blue and gold finish line arch looming in the distance. The cheers grew louder and louder - there was no stopping at that point. "Come on, come on," I told myself, then 100 yards left. All I could think was "Oh my God, I am going to finish the Boston Marathon." I crossed the finish line, grinning from ear to ear, as I watched my dream come true.

Finishing time: 3:38:51(8:21/mile pace)

Overall place: 9,723/22,540

So much joy. And then quickly, so much pain. The body can endure running a marathon but once it's over, suddenly even walking becomes hard. I took 6-inch steps as I shuffled my way toward picking up my finisher's medal. I found my parents, and received many hugs from them.

Once we got back to the hotel, my parents, who are healthy and in good shape, looked visibly uncomfortable. Standing in the same spot in 50-degree weather since 7 a.m. caused them to stiffen up. They waited at the finish line, pressed up against other spectators, for that one fleeting moment as I ran by. I laughed as I watched my dad stretch his legs as if he was the one who ran 26.2 miles. I'm fairly confident that they would've waited outside for 12 hours in snow to watch me race.

The next morning, there were many marathoners at the airport. We all wore our finisher medals as we slowly waddled through security: still feeling the effects of the race. As I boarded my flight, the flight attendant asked me how the race went and then jotted something on a notepad. After we were settled in our seats, the flight attendant came on the intercom,

"Yesterday was the Boston Marathon, a race that brings together some of the best runners in the world to run 26.2 miles. Today, we have a number of marathon finishers on our flight to D.C., and we want to acknowledge their tremendous accomplishment. In seat 5B..."

She proceeded to list each of us by name. As people clapped for each of us, I held back tears. The warm wishes and congratulations from my seatmates made me feel like an Olympian and that my finisher's medal was a gold medal. Boston treats all of its runners like winners. Finishing was one of the greatest accomplishments of my life, and I was on cloud 9.

Chapter 5: An Uphill Battle

"Don't try to rush progress. Remember - a step forward,
no matter how small, is a step in the right direction."
– Kara Goucher, 2007 World Silver Medalist

I returned to D.C. so visibly thrilled from my Boston Marathon debut that Dr. Jansen asked if there was a way to bottle that joy. The marathon sustained me for weeks after, and made the end of the semester more bearable. I still had a great deal of work to do, but was filled with the knowledge that I had accomplished something that my professors and classmates viewed as a challenging endeavor. It made me determined to keep my head down and focus on the task ahead.

On Wednesdays, there was an hour gap between my history classes. Eager to get some fresh air, I often prepared for the second class in the plaza outside of our department. It was peaceful and free from any distractions. As I thumbed through my notes, one of the history professors passed by, and yelled out "Congratulations!" Confused, I put away my notebook and ran up to him. "Professor West, what do you mean?" I asked, uncertain about his well wishes. "You didn't hear?" he said, not realizing that he was the bearer of good news, "Oh, I guess the announcement hasn't gone out yet. The department made their decisions on TAs for next year. We're excited that you'll be one of them."

"Oh! I had no idea! Well, this is great news...thank you!" I stammered, full of relief that I didn't have to take out more student loans. Professor West continued on his way, and I pretended to return to my notebook until he was out of earshot, trying to preserve a shred of professional decorum. I called my parents to tell them the good news. This conversation was as tearful as when I had told them that I didn't get the Lilly Fellowship, but instead of crying in defeat, I shed tears of joy.

***

While some master's degrees conclude with a thesis paper, my program culminated with two days of comprehensive exams, also known as comps. Although there is no real hazing in graduate school, there is some fondness among senior graduate students and professors to regale the younger students with their own comps stories. They bragged about their staggering lists of required reading and tough exam questions, all the while assuring us that we would do "just fine."

The task was to read 60 books from four categories: Byzantine History, Early Western Medieval History, Late Western Medieval History, and Early Modern History. The test consisted of two four-hour days of writing essays. The exams were designed to test my ability to synthesize the arguments and prove my mastery over the historiographical debates. Failure was not an option – I had been conditionally accepted into the Ph.D. program, pending completion of this final test.

The bulk of my studying took place while I worked as an administrator for The Center for Talented Youth (CTY): an academic summer camp for gifted teenagers at Skidmore College in Saratoga Springs, NY. Studying required long hours on top of an already-busy schedule. After work, I worked on practice essays about early Christian burials, changes in the English monarchy, the iconoclasm controversies of the Orthodox Church, and the consequences of the Reformation. I carried my flashcards everywhere, asking anyone who was willing to quiz me.

That included my younger sibling Nova, who I was ecstatic to have joining me for the summer. It was fun to partake in a new adventure together - we had never really done anything together as adults. Sometimes I needed a break from the drama of my staff. Nova and I would grab dinner, which gave us the opportunity to gossip about the camp. We even performed a goofy dance number in the program's talent show, much to the amusement of the staff and students.

The history department let me take the exam in Saratoga Spring, which meant I didn't have to travel back to D.C. for the exam. Instead, I was locked in a colleague's office in New York without the internet while I wrote essays on Byzantine and early medieval history. One question that asked to define the chronological boundaries of the early Middle Ages led to me constructing an argument that centered around the reign of Charlemagne and the ensuing rulers who sought to model their kingdoms after his. In this deep dive, I addressed changing practices of kingship and the various scholarly debates centered around this topic. I finished the first day in about 3 hours and 40 minutes: about the same amount of time it took me to run a marathon. It truly felt like a mental marathon: it required months of preparation and also caused a feeling of exhaustion afterwards.

As I had done on Day 1 of comps, I went for an early morning run, listening to certain psych-up songs as I mentally prepared for the test. That summer, Kesha's "Your Love is My Drug" was one of the big hits, and it put me in a good mood every time I heard it. The song got me pumped up for track workouts, and it also worked similar magic on Test Day. As I opened the envelope that revealed the second day's essay questions, I smiled. The exam asked thorough questions that I knew I could answer. I frantically typed out outlines for each essay, which then turned into detailed arguments about the historiographical intricacies of each field. One essay asked how humanists from the Italian Renaissance sought to distinguish themselves from the people of the newly-coined "Middle Ages." As I sketched out my response, I discussed how changes in the university curriculum, namely, the shift from the scholastic movement to what is now known as the liberal arts education, created a clear contrast between the two historical periods. With an hour to go, I kept repeating to myself, "Hang in, hold on, finish strong," using my marathon mental strategies to help succeed in school.

A few days later, I received a message from the department that I passed. It was a big stepping-stone in my academic career.

But an entire doctoral program still loomed ahead of me. The shadow of my multiple struggles with Latin made me wonder what other potential difficulties awaited me in the Ph.D. program.

***

CTY ended in early August, and I headed back to Washington to start my first semester as a doctoral student. I moved into my first apartment: a two-bedroom apartment in Takoma Park that I shared with Julie, a fellow grad student in the history department. When we first moved in together in August 2010, all we had in common was that we were both aspiring historians and in need of a roommate. Within a few months, Julie became one of my closest friends. The two years that we were roommates gave me some of the best memories from grad school. Our conversations that began after we finished our homework in the evening often continued well into the night.

I was excited to start my new role as a Teaching Assistant and finally stand in front of the classroom and lead weekly discussions with my students. I also quickly dove into the trenches and learned how to grade papers and provide students with effective feedback designed to stimulate their academic development.

I was also gearing up for the upcoming Rochester Marathon. I trained all summer, continuing to follow Sarah's plans to a T, and hoped that I could have a great race in my hometown in September. Through August, my workouts went well, and I was optimistic about another PR.

***

As I wrapped my weekly track workout at the end of August, the top of my left foot hurt. I ignored it: chalking it up to an off day. But on the next day's run, the discomfort was back. Wanting to be cautious, I took the next day off from running. I propped up and iced my foot whenever I wasn't in class. I started to panic, wondering, "What is causing this pain? Why is this happening so close to the marathon?" I had never experienced a problem like this.

I decided to take yet another day off, hoping that the back-to-back rest days would help. I also got a massage: needing some relief from all of the shoulder tension that came from hunching over my books for comps. The masseur kneaded out the tension in my shoulders and upper back. He also rubbed out some of the "gravel" in my feet - knots had built up. There was no pain when he rubbed my left foot, and he said I had a good range of motion.

But despite the rest and massage, my foot hurt every time I ran, even if it was just for three miles. The knot in my stomach grew as race day drew nearer - was this a stress fracture? That meant months off from running. I had looked at pictures of feet all weekend on WebMD, foolishly trying to self-diagnose the problem. I saw Sarah the Monday before the race to get her opinion on how to proceed. She asked, "Does it feel like your shoes are tied too tight, even when they're not?" That's exactly how it felt, which caused Sarah to conclude, "It's tendonitis - you can run on that. Get through the marathon, and then we can reassess." I sighed in relief. Although it wasn't ideal to run a marathon feeling uncomfortable, it was doable. I knew I'd likely need to reevaluate things afterward – perhaps take some extended time off. Although I did not feel 100%, I knew I'd give it my all on race day.

***

The night before the race, I had made my peace with my foot - it was time to relax and go to bed. While a single good night's sleep can't produce a good race, a bad night's sleep can easily ruin a race. I managed to get seven hours of sleep, and even when I woke up at 2 a.m., I rolled back over and promptly fell back asleep. My parents drove me to the start of the race, and once again, I was sitting in the backseat making the trek downtown that we did hundreds of times growing up. Before the start of the race, I ran into a bunch of old friends from my childhood. Chatting with them kept me relaxed and ready to go.

Given that it was a smaller race, I didn't have to jockey to get into a comfortable position. There was a group of five guys running right in front of me. I let them block me from the wind and let their conversations wash over me. Although it was drizzling, the light rain felt refreshing. Around mile 5, I realized that I needed to let the man-pack go, at least for now. I didn't want to press the pace too hard early in the race. Although my foot bothered me, I tried to dismiss the pain. "Relax," I thought, "you've already run more comfortably than you thought, you can do this."

Then at mile 9, the course veered onto the Erie Canal – one of the most historic landmarks in Rochester. I have always loved the Erie Canal. I grew up on it, biked on it, went for walks on it, and when I started running, trained on it. Things grew quiet over the next 12 miles: the pack had thinned out, and there were spectators every few hundred yards. With the familiarity of the path, I tried to imagine that I was out on a long run, not in the middle of a marathon. I relaxed a bit, knew I could manage the pain in my foot, and took in the surroundings. The air was damp and had that wet smell of nature, which I found calming. Spectators popped up here and there. One woman shouted, "Go little girl!" and I yelled back, "I'm not little, I'm 24!" causing the other runners to laugh.

At 13 miles, I picked things up and passed a few people who I had had my eye on for miles. One of the advantages about running on the Erie Canal, which had no turns, was that I could clearly see who was ahead and by how much. It was time to reel the man-pack I had let go of 15 miles before. With a new-found surge of confidence, I passed them in one fell swoop. At the 20-mile mark, it was time to be tenacious. I had opened up a gap between some of the runners. As I appeared from around a bend, spectators clapped and yelled "you're one of the fastest women in the race!"

I had never trained so I had never had such actual pain during a marathon. But the nauseous feeling I normally had around mile 20 was not there.

Mile 23 finally appeared. Even though my foot was aching, it was time to accelerate. We were back in downtown Rochester and the people were out in full force. "Go, go," I thought.

Thoughts of the pain started to vanish away. I could see my parents as I headed down the home stretch. This was my hometown, my marathon, my advantage, and I finished strong as I crossed the finish line.

My parents immediately enveloped me in a big hug. They had been so worried about my foot issues that they even tried to convince me not to start the race or drop out if the pain was too much. Instead, they were excited to watch me finish with a smile on my face.

Finishing time: 3:35:54 (8:13/mile)

Overall place: 115/573

10th place for women (10/203)

Age group (19-24): 3rd

I was doubly excited about placing in my age group and finishing in the top 10 female finishers. I didn't do anything stupid in this race: I didn't blast off in the first half, and my patience was rewarded later on in the race.

***

On Halloween 2010, I had the opportunity to run the Marine Corps Marathon side by side with Jenny – a friend of mine from CTY. This race was seven weeks after my own Rochester Marathon, but I figured that since there would be such a disparity in pace, going from 8:15 miles to approximately 9:00 miles, my body would hold up. After a few weeks of recovering from the Rochester Marathon, I did a couple of long runs to make sure that my body could endure another marathon. The foot pain I had experienced in September largely went away, and I dismissed it as a fluke.

Jenny flew in from Florida and we had a blast palling around D.C. the day before the race. The memories of my first marathon were still fresh, and I could sense her excitement about her own debut. As we made our way to the start, I felt full of joy being able to share this experience with a dear friend. As we waited for the race to begin, we hugged one last time, and with a resounding blast of the military cannon, we were off!

Although the early miles were lighthearted and fun, in the

final miles of the race, it was clear that the cumulative miles had taken a toll on Jenny. I did my best to do whatever I could to keep her going and put one foot in front of the other: singing, cheering, yelling words of encouragement. Her time goal was well within reach, and I started yelling "Come on, come on!" as we trudged onward. I could tell how exhausted Jenny was, even though she was close to the finish and the Marines were cheering her on. As we ascended that final steep hill, I grabbed her hand, and we crossed the finish line in 3:57:38.

In the course of a year, Jenny went from a new runner excited about running a 5k to someone about to try to run a marathon. Amazing things can happen when two friends work together to make the seemingly impossible a reality.

***

All semester, I felt exhausted. Maybe it was running two marathons seven weeks apart. Or perhaps it was the combination of beginning the doctoral program and holding down two part-time jobs. My mind and body were operating in overdrive and the pace was no longer sustainable.

That October, my aunt Barbara was diagnosed with Celiac Disease, an autoimmune disorder that prevents the body from absorbing nutrients. Because Celiac is genetic, my mom insisted that all of us take a blood test to rule it out. I vehemently protested: there was no way I had something wrong with me. Besides, at my most recent physical, my doctor proclaimed me to be one of his healthiest patients. I begrudgingly went to the lab.

A week later, I was getting ready to go to a holiday party when the phone rang. I picked it up without thinking – it was my physician. "Vanessa, you do have Celiac. I'm going to get you set up with a specialist when you come home for Christmas. They'll be able to do some scans and help you figure out your new diet." I mumbled "thank you," and quickly got off the phone. My immediate reaction was one of denial. I was a marathon runner: how could I have a disease that was breaking down my body?

A few minutes later, Wes came over to pick me up for the party, surprised to find me in tears. I explained what happened and tried to put on a bright face. When we arrived to our friend's house, I was surrounded by all of the foods I'd soon be saying goodbye to. It felt like torture.

After a few days of wallowing, I found some perspective. This was not cancer: I was not going to die. My diagnosis was more of a warning. I needed to radically change my diet; otherwise, I'd someday face osteoporosis, infertility, and even intestinal cancer.

In researching Celiac Disease, I learned that one of the symptoms is fatigue: something I had experienced for much of my adult life. But that seemed easy to attribute to both marathon training and being a full-time grad student. Even when I got a full night's sleep, I often woke up still exhausted. Perhaps this was why.

I learned about Amy Yoder Begley: a professional distance runner who was diagnosed with Celiac in 2006. She said that since she found out, the diagnosis made a big difference in her performance and overall quality of life: "I've actually found that energy levels are much better during the day. I'm not having a lot of lows anymore and I feel better." After learning how to manage her diagnosis, Amy competed in the 2008 Beijing Olympics in the 10,000 meters.

Learning Amy's story gave me hope and made me wonder, had I been running on partial capacity? I needed to focus on this possibility, rather than the foods I had to give up. Maybe this change in diet would give me more energy and allow me to run faster. It also helped to explain my complicated relationship with food.

Since I was a child, I found everything surrounding mealtime to be a stressful experience. I was a picky kid, and I only had a small set of staple dishes that I enjoyed. Going out to dinner, while a treat for most, was an anxious occasion for me, as I wondered if I'd like anything on the menu. Once restaurant menus became available online, I carefully examined the menu beforehand in order to have some idea as to what to order.

My mom often made pasta on evenings when we had to

eat quickly, and the fact that I had to rush through the meal that bothered my stomach exacerbated the situation. Even when we got pizza, popular with most kids, I asked my mom for a big salad to accompany it, and barely finished one slice.

Trying to process the diagnosis, I realized a lot of the meals that I didn't tolerate were loaded with bread. Was my body trying to tell me something? Following my diagnosis, my parents felt guilty, because for years they had tried to cajole me into eating more. But growing up in the 90s, Celiac was not well known, and my doctor, though he was well-aware of my aversion to eating most foods, never suggested getting tested for it.

I tried to use running to cope with the fact that I needed to upend my entire diet. But my left knee hurt every time I ran. Even if I took a few days off, the pain came back. Although Celiac and the knee problems weren't related, I felt that my body was failing me in every respect. The Boston Marathon was four months away: I didn't want to drop out of the greatest race in the world. Even worse, I worried that I'd never be able to run a marathon again.

Christmas break was a blur of doctors' visits. Between the preliminary meeting with the GI specialist, the endoscopy to confirm the diagnosis, the follow-up, the meeting with the nutritionist, the X-Rays to rule out any stress fractures, I went to eight appointments in two weeks. The endoscopy showed that my damaged intestines were the equivalent of a smoker's lungs. I was going to have to completely change what kinds of food I consumed. "Vanessa, you're going to have to be completely vigilant with what you put in your body," the dietician told me. "Any time you go to a party or restaurant, you need to make it clear to everyone that there cannot be any cross-contamination with your food." I felt overwhelmed – I was already anxious when eating in public. I dreaded having to carefully discuss meal options with waiters and party hosts every time I went out. But as the doctors and dieticians assured me, while Celiac was a life sentence (could they use a less gloomy term?), it was manageable.

The orthopedist diagnosed the knee pain as ITBS (iliotibial band syndrome). She referred me to a physical therapist to strengthen my knee and help me return to running. I was not sure if the Boston Marathon was remained a possibility in April. As it was time to ring in 2011, I hoped the New Year would mean an end to the pain and usher in a new era of opportunities.

Chapter 6: Fixing What's Broken

"Get going. Get up and walk if you have to, but finish the
damned race." – Ron Hill, 1970 Boston Marathon Champion

I returned to D.C. in January with two important lists: a
list of acceptable and forbidden foods, and a series of physical
therapy exercises to help with the ITBS. On my first day back in
Washington, I managed to run four slow miles without any knee
pain. I hadn't had a pain-free run in over a month. I was excited
to enjoy a run without any discomfort. But would I be ready to
run Boston in April?

After emailing Sarah about my Celiac diagnosis and the IT
band issues, she replied,

*"I agree that you will need to alter your marathon training,
but that is not necessarily a bad thing. Here is a general outline of
what I think would be fantastic training:*

*Cycle 1: Focus on "base" training. Run four days a week and
do cross-training and strength work three days a week. For example,
Tues, Thurs, Sat and Sun would be runs. Monday, Wednesday and
Friday would be cross-training days with strength/core work after.
If you could do "doubles" these days, I think that would be an excellent way to get extra aerobic "mileage" for the marathon. So, if
you were able to swim in the mornings and then do 45-60 minutes
of cardio (bike or elliptical) in the afternoon/evening that would be
great. After the afternoon/evening session, tack on a 20-30-minute
strength/core/stretching session.*

*I bet with the new gluten free diet and all of the new strength/
cross training; you'll actually feel really revitalized! Let's go Boston
2011!*

Feeling excited about Sarah's plan, I optimistically journaled about the upcoming changes.

***

January 20, 2011

Today is a fresh start.

Today is the first day of classes. I already had one class (a directed readings course on early medieval religion), which was a lot of fun. It is only Dr. Davis and me: it is like a personalized and vigorous book club. It is nice to finally be able to have an advanced, intellectual conversation about good books – this would have freaked me out a year ago.

Today is my first day on the gluten-free diet. I had pizza and beer last night as a "last hurrah," and will start things anew today. Today also kicks off two weeks of base training before marathon training starts on the 24th. This afternoon, I am going to swim 2000 yards, and then get on the elliptical this evening after class.

I'm vowing to be more optimistic about these lifestyle changes. I started the new diet today to coincide with the beginning of the new semester. The gastroenterologist said a year of eating gluten-free will hopefully clear the damage. Additionally, my physical therapist told me that even within four weeks, physical therapy can repair IT band damage. I'm trying to be hopeful that this plan will help change my body from the inside out.

***

To rehab my knee, twice a day I needed to do a series of dynamic exercises and balancing activities. It took about a half hour to get through the whole set, which added in an extra hour of strength work each day – more than I had ever done on a regular basis. In the morning, I watched the early morning local news as I balanced on one foot or did a series of lunges with various resistance bands. At the end of the day, I caught up with my roommate Julie as I completed my physical therapy.

Three times a week, I cross-trained twice a day, supplemented by weight training. On cross-training days, I woke up around 5 a.m. I had to be out the door by 6:30 to catch the metro and be there when the pool opened at 7 a.m. I swam for 45 minutes, and then did weights for 30 minutes. Then I showered, went to classes and work, and then in the afternoon hopped on the elliptical or rowing machine. I had completely diversified my training regimen and was on the road to becoming the strongest I had ever been in my life.

I carefully followed the recommendations for the gluten-free diet. At the grocery store, I closely read all the labels for products that said "gluten-free" as well as "this product is not manufactured on equipment containing wheat or gluten products." When I went out to eat, I always spoke to the manager to learn whether the menu items that were listed as "gluten-free" were prepared in a dedicated space, in order to avoid any cross-contamination. When a salad arrived with croutons, after I had clearly indicated that I had Celiac, my face immediately turned red with embarrassment when I knew I'd need to send the dish back. I felt incredibly self-conscious as all eyes turned on me, suddenly grinding the conversation to a halt. I worried that I came off as overbearing when in reality, I was trying to remain healthy.

One night, after getting home late from teaching, I ordered a gluten-free pizza. When the pizza arrived, I quickly wolfed down a few slices, and then returned to grade a stack of papers. I had gotten through the first few papers when my stomach lurched. I ran to the bathroom, barely making it before I began to vomit uncontrollably.

This wasn't the flu, nor was it from drinking. I had been "glutened" - I had accidentally and unwittingly ingested the food I had worked to keep out of my system. The restaurant must've overlooked my request to make the pizza gluten-free. After completely eliminating gluten from my diet, my body revolted at this foreign substance like it was poisonous. For the next few hours, I remained hunched over the porcelain throne. When there was literally nothing left in my system, I crawled into bed. It was miserable. Yet, the episode justified me being more persnickety when ordering food in public settings – mistakes like that came at a real cost.

I was testing my body in ways and was hungry for evidence that the new diet and running plan were working.

**

In early February, I signed up for a local eight-mile race to test the state of my fitness. Sarah thought I could run eight miles in an hour (7:30 pace). I was less than convinced - the pace seemed to be beyond my ability.

While I warmed up, the doubts continued. As I jogged, I wondered whether my legs were ready to aggressively accelerate when it was time to race. I needed to push the doubts aside and turn to positive thinking. At check-in, I bumped into Heather, another runner who I met through a Boston Marathon online forum. As we chatted while waiting to start, we thought that we would finish around the same time.

Heather and I quickly fell into stride together and decided that we ought to try to run the whole race together and see what happens. We went through the first mile in 6:53. *Oh my goodness - that is faster than my best 5k pace!* 2 miles in 13:55. At this point, Heather speculated, "Well, we are either going to run a killer race or have a killer crash-and-burn." We decided to go for broke, and push each other through the hard parts. We went through the 5k in 21:46 – I had achieved a new 5k PR in the middle of an 8-mile race.

At the halfway point, the wind picked up and it started to feel like a really hard run. At the 10k mark Heather deadpanned, "I think we have our sub-hour in the bag." The combination of the fast pace and running straight into a headwind was challenging. Heather had gained five yards on me, and I could not catch up. The minutes went by slowly, but finally, the finish line appeared. I crossed in 57:40 – 7:12 pace for eight miles.

It was a phenomenal race and offered me confirmation that my new form of training was working. This was one of my best performances to date. All I needed to do was trust in the plan, and with ten weeks to go, I felt more hopeful about Boston than I had in months.

**

In addition to the performance benefits I was seeing on the road, I was honing in on my academics at the same time. Perhaps it was the rigorousness of the running schedule that made me treat my coursework with added intensity. One class in particular that semester fundamentally changed the trajectory of my academic career.

I came to CUA interested in studying the later Middle Ages, roughly 1100-1500. There were many things I found fascinating about the period: the Crusades, the Black Death, and the rich and varied expressions of Christian spirituality. Despite the rocky end to my senior thesis in college, I wanted to keep writing about the 1324 witch trial of Alice Kyteler. Because of my curiosity to learn more about it continued well into graduate school, I naively decided that it should also become my dissertation topic.

Thankfully, my professors at Catholic kept their reservations about this particular subject to themselves. Instead, they encouraged me to immerse myself in coursework that broadly considered the topic of medieval religious history. I happily obliged, because I was fascinated with the Christian culture of pilgrimage, saints, prayer practices, and other religious traditions that developed in the Middle Ages. As a lifelong Catholic, it was interesting to learn more about how different devotional practices that became central to Catholicism emerged during the historical period I loved.

To ensure that I was a well-rounded medievalist, I had to take classes both in early and late medieval history. Dr. Jennifer Davis, the department's early medieval historian, offered to lead a directed reading course with me, entitled "Early Medieval Monasticism, Sanctity, and Piety." Dr. Davis, a Harvard-educated professor, was one of the smartest people I had ever met, and already had achieved a great deal of success before she had even obtained tenure. She had an innate ability to ask probing questions and to challenge her students to think critically. Each Monday morning, we met in her office to discuss the book we had both read. It was both one of the most challenging and rewarding hours of the week. The accountability that came with being the lone student made me a better thinker and historian.

I was intrigued by the fascinating books that we read together, such as *Furta Sacra: Thefts of Relics in the Central Middle Ages* by Patrick Geary. This particular book examined why some people (and even entire towns) sought to steal precious relics - significant objects related to a particular saint. For example, I was surprised to learn that the body of Mary Magdalene was allegedly stolen from the French town of Provence and moved to Vézelay. This movement of her relics sparked an influx of pilgrims who wished to visit the bones of one of Jesus's earliest followers. I often left class with my head spinning with questions. After our discussion on *Furta Sacra*, I talked endlessly about the class with my roommate Julie over dinner. In between bites, she remarked, "You know, Vanessa, you've never spoken with that kind of excitement when you've talked about medieval witchcraft."

I spent all weekend thinking about Julie's observation. What would happen if, in my last semester of coursework, I abandoned one topic in favor a dissimilar project? Would I have to stay in graduate school even longer than I anticipated? The average doctoral program takes about seven years to complete - I did not want to extend my program. While I found the potential change to be overwhelming, I was also on an academic high as I thought about some of the potential topics I could study in the field of medieval religious history: pilgrimage, saints' cults, relic practices, etc. On Monday, I asked Dr. Davis for advice. I told her that I was titillated by our reading, and that it made me question whether I was studying the right topic.

While carefully listening, Dr. Davis quickly put together some books that could pique my interests, as well as a few potential research topics to keep in mind. Additionally, she encouraged me to take some time to think about this, and then to reach out to Dr. Jansen, who was on sabbatical in Italy. A few days later, I wrote her an email explaining what I had been studying all semester, and that I was considering making a drastic shift in my studies,

This excitement and passion has led me to contemplate leaving behind the witchcraft project and picking this up as a new dissertation topic. I am excited about what lies ahead.

I was nervous about her reaction. In the three years that I had already spent at CUA, Dr. Jansen had already invested a lot of her time in me. In reality, my change in topic was well received, as her research also focused on medieval religious culture. Filled with anticipation, I waited for her response,

Now is the time to switch. The most important thing in choosing a dissertation project is that you are genuinely interested in the topic as this interest has to sustain you for years to come.

***

March 12, 2011

In less than two months, the starting pistol will go off and I will set off on my dream race. Lately, I have trained with what I think is a new intensity and passion. I have a new goal in mind: sub 3:30. In the past, I have been hesitant to set big goals, in part because I don't want to fail and disappoint myself. But I now have two years of marathon training under my belt, and over a year of more focused training through Sarah's guidance. And now, I am staring into the distance, imagining Hopkinton, Ashland, Natick, Wellesley, Newton, Brookline, and finally, the promise of Boston that awaits me.

I have run Boston before. I know what Heartbreak Hill feels like. But how will it feel if I step outside of myself, dig deep, push myself, reach and find that new layer?

I could make my dreams come true.

In order for me to succeed in Boston, a number of things need to come together:

- *I need to maintain my nutrition. I have come to find a lot of great foods that help fuel my runs and aid in my recovery. I think I eat better in general. I don't drink as much. I don't splurge on fast food, since I don't necessarily know if there's gluten in a product that probably isn't good for me anyways. It must be working.*
- *I need to maintain consistency with my cross training. It is hard doing double days of cross training, and I don't get that*

same thrill of a 5 a.m. alarm to go rowing or swimming that I do for running. But there are only six weeks to go – I can keep swimming for a little longer.

- *I need to keep doing some strength training and continue to do my rehab exercises. These are all of the ancillary things that can make a major difference.*

- *I need to trust the process. I need to believe that this plan will work. Sarah trains with people who have gone to the Olympic Trials and the track workouts I do are modified versions of theirs.*

- *I know how to step outside of myself. The Freezeroo 8 miler was a signal that I am ready for a breakthrough. I am getting better at pushing myself and feeling more comfortable being uncomfortable.*

- *I need to run with joy. I gain strength from my family and friends, and I need to harness that. I had an amazing weekend at Kathleen and Sandeep's wedding this weekend. That joy even translated into my long run the following day. I ran 19 miles on the treadmill, averaging 8:18 pace. That is solid for a long run, considering long runs are supposed to be about 45 seconds slower than race pace. This should mean that 8-minute miles should feel relatively comfortable. Even though it was mentally challenging to stay focused on the treadmill for almost three hours, in some ways, I know it will be easier in Boston. I'll have changes in scenery, and I'll have people cheering for me and supporting me.*

- *I have the tools in hand, a brand-new body that I myself have rebuilt, and a support system that will be there for me along the way.*

This is an achievable dream.

Now is the time.

I was hungry for a breakthrough performance on race day.

***

Two minutes into the 2011 Boston Marathon, I looked down and realized that I did not start my watch! "How could I forget to do this? How am I going to figure out my time?"

I wondered, my brain trying to come up with a solution. The adrenaline over my mistake caused my heart rate to accelerate - I needed to calm down. After scrambling for ideas, I decided I would start my watch at the one-mile mark, and then use the "lap" function on my watch for every mile and run according to feel. As I went through my first timed mile in 7:25, I told myself, "Whoa, easy girl. No need to make up for any imagined lost time yet." Within a few miles, I had evened out to 7:45 pace.

I was in the zone, running stride for stride with a woman of similar stature, and we even both had orange tops on. Although we didn't speak to each other while we were running, it was as if we were offering silent encouragement to each other. This shared solidarity lasted for a few miles, and then, we lost each other among the masses.

Other than giving some kids high fives, I tried to focus and maintain a steady pace. I took advantage of the families who set up water stops on their front lawns, as the temperature was quickly rising. I kept dumping water on my head at every opportunity. I drank water or Gatorade at almost every stop: I figured it was best to be overcautious with hydration on a warmer day.

It was unnerving to not know my overall time. My thoughts keep going back and forth from "Is this too fast?" to "I could totally go faster, but I won't." The screams from the girls at Wellesley College started to rumble in the distance. "Brace yourself, listen to them, and harness their energy for later," I told myself. I could feel their screams vibrating on my skin. After Wellesley, the next few miles clicked off quickly. I hoped my pace strategy would not backfire. "Maybe I can pick it up after Heartbreak, but I can't press the pace until then," as I tried to rationally reel myself in.

With ten miles to go, I started to feel tired for the first time in the race. When I made the first turn of the course, the spectators were out and ready to help get us ready to climb these hills. After climbing the first of the three Newton hills, I ran my first mile over eight-minute pace. "That's okay, these hills are hard: you need to go easy."

I was hot and tired with nine miles to go, and it was time for Heartbreak Hill. I had trained on harder hills and I was ready for this. It is a long climb, and patience is a necessity to make it to the top. When I finally had reached the top of Heartbreak Hill, the frat boys of Boston College were waiting and cheering. Yet, I felt my energy dipping. Although dropping out never entered my mind, the urge to sit down on the curb to rest kept popping into my head. I tried to push that idea aside. I knew that if I stopped moving, it would be nearly impossible to start running again. Coupled with the fact that I wasn't totally sure of my overall time, I felt unfocused, bordering on discombobulated.

My mind became a jumble of fuzzy thoughts and images. I had never felt that exhausted in a marathon before. "Get down to three miles, then you have less than half an hour of running left," I instructed myself, trying to picture what Sarah would say if she were running next to me. As we ran alongside a set of trolley tracks in Brookline, people on the trolleys were leaning out the windows and taking pictures of us. "We're dying out here and they're photographing it?" I half-indignantly wondered, as my thoughts swirled into a haze of confusion. The spectators' cheers sounded like they were yelling in slow-motion. Someone near me ran with an American flag, causing people to chant "USA! USA! USA!" My heart surged with a burst of patriotic pride. As the crowd chanted, I felt myself getting excited again: the cheers provided a resurgence of energy.

My heart was pounding with two miles to go. "You can get through another mile, and then it's one to go. Keep your head down, ignore the Citgo sign, and keep going…How are there more hills?" Then, I glimpsed the Citgo 1-mile to go sign. "Come on, Vanessa, you can do this, you have trained for months for this moment." It was time to make the final turn to get onto the most famous street in marathoning.

The blue finish arch hung like a glimmering beacon of hope. The energy of the crowd was indescribable. I knew that along with thousands of other people, my parents were somewhere in the stands. I looked to my left with 100 yards to go, and miraculously, despite not wearing my glasses, I could see them clearly. I joyfully waved to them and continued on. I crossed the finish line, doing what a few months before seemed impossible.

And because I didn't start my watch at the beginning of the race, I had no idea what time I finished in.

I collected my cape and medal, and then trudged over to my school bus to pick up the gear I had checked. Somehow, the woman in the orange top from the beginning of the race materialized again – we must've finished around the same time. As we waited in line to pick up our bags, the two of us leaned on each other in mutual exhaustion. Although we were able to demonstrate athletic prowess just minutes before, we needed each other to remain upright. We muttered words of congratulations to each other, then became silent as fatigue fell over us. Although we never exchanged names, there is a special bond that forms when participating in an arduous challenge.

I could barely walk. I shuffled to the curb and sat down. I called my parents, who gleefully reported my time:

Finishing time: 3:27:00 (7:54 per mile)

Overall: 6,764/23,879

"Oh my God, I did it," I yelled to my parents over the phone. It was almost a 9-minute PR, and a 12-minute improvement from the previous year's Boston. The diet, the cross training: it all paid off. I went sub 3:30 with room to spare.

***

When I got back to D.C., I found the letter I had written to myself six weeks before the marathon. Reading it again, it almost felt prophetic and this line put a lump in my throat,

This is an achievable dream. Now is the time.

I had put so much time in rehabbing my knee in order to return to Boston. All of those hours in the pool, doing stretches around the apartment at 5 a.m., slowly making my way back to running, were done in the hope of being able to run pain-free. Finishing this race wasn't just a triumph: but a reward for all of that hard work.

It really was an achievable dream.

Chapter 7: Growth Spurts

"We all have dreams. But in order to make dreams come into reality, it takes an awful lot of determination, dedication, self-discipline, and effort."
– Jesse Owens, 1936 Olympic Gold Medalist

My Boston PR indicated that I was in the middle of a running growth spurt. Having strung together several successful years of training, I was stretching the bounds of what I thought was possible in running. In a similar vein, I was experiencing a growth spurt in grad school. I was nearly done with my first year in the Ph.D. program, and felt more confident in myself and excited about my career path.

In addition to my classes, I was a TA for a class on early medieval Rome, c. 400-800. This class was co-taught by two dynamic professors: my directed studies professor, Dr. Davis, and Dr. Philip Rousseau, who could only be described as an academic Sir Ian McKellen. Dr. Rousseau was one of the titans of the history of late antiquity and adored by faculty and students alike. His quick wit and off-the-cuff remarks in his British accent set us off into fits of laughter. At first glance, the two professors seemed to be completely opposite of each other: Dr. Davis was short and young, Dr. Rousseau was tall and in his late 70s, she taught early medieval history, he taught late antiquity. Each day, they heatedly debated the changing status of Rome after the end of the Roman Empire. As the TAs for the class, my friends Wes, Carol, and I, sat in the back of the auditorium at the edge of our seats, gleefully watching them in action. We chided our students, "Do you realize how lucky you are to study with these professors?" trying to underscore to them that this was a unique opportunity to be in the presence of such renowned academics.

After we had finished grading final exams, Dr. Davis and Dr. Rousseau took us TAs out for a celebratory dinner. As we enjoyed Mediterranean cuisine and fine wine, we reminisced about the class and delved into rich topics of medieval history, probing our professors about their research plans for the summer. Once the plates were cleared, our professors toasted each of us. When I got home that night, I wrote down what Dr. Davis said to me,

"Vanessa, you have transformed so much since you started at CUA, and that has been lovely to watch."

I often opened my journal to the page that had Dr. Davis's comment during moments of doubt to remember that she, a professor I admired so much, had faith in me.

**

Sarah was pleased with how Boston went, but suggested that I consider stepping away from the marathon for a time: "Vanessa, you know how to maintain a pace that won't make you collapse in a marathon, and while that's good, you need to learn how to push outside of your comfort zone and learn what it feels like to hang on in a shorter race when it feels painfully fast." She said that I should consider developing some short-term leg speed and focus on distances ranging from 5k to the half marathon. Doing so would make me a stronger runner with a broader range of ability.

We continued to use the basic training structure that had proven to be successful, but my long runs topped out around 15 miles. Additionally, my track workouts and tempo runs were completed at a faster pace. In 2011, I changed my diet, training, and academic area of research. Each adjustment helped me to become more open to taking on the unknown.

**

For five summers, I worked at the Center for Talented Youth site in Saratoga Springs, NY. I had many great memories there: going to Uncommon Grounds for coffee and board games on Sunday afternoons with my colleagues or enjoying a couple of cheap drinks at the local dive bar, Desperate Annie's, at the end of a long day. I loved the charm of this horse-racing town and was able to take on a leadership position as a junior administrator. In 2010, my supervisor Stella, the academic dean of the site, started to show me the ropes of her daily workload so that I could apply for a dean-level position the following summer at one of the dozen sites around the country. While I had hoped to eventually move through the ranks of the administration, I wasn't sure if I was ready to take on a more difficult set of responsibilities, as well as supervise a large staff at a young age.

Following a two-hour interview with questions on pedagogy, learning styles, faculty management, and emergency protocol, I was offered the position of academic dean at CTY Santa Cruz in California. I was initially overwhelmed about the prospect of living on the West Coast all summer. I had never even traveled west of Indiana: California seemed utterly foreign. My parents reminded me that I could work 300 miles away from loved ones or 3,000 miles and three time zones: it wouldn't make a difference. Once again, I decided to step out of my comfort zone, and flew out to Santa Cruz to begin the summer program on June 19th – my 25th birthday.

As the plane descended into the San José International Airport, I was immediately awestruck by the majestic beauty of California. The mountains dwarfed any natural landscape I had ever seen. When I stepped outside to ride to campus with Mike, our program manager, the air felt different. It was refreshingly cool, as if I could drink it in. The sky was bright blue, and although the sun was shining, the temperature barely reached 60 degrees. I was accustomed to 90 degrees and humidity in Washington: Northern California was a welcome change.

While Mike pointed out the local sights, I sat in the passenger seat with my face nearly pressed against the window as I took in the imposing mountains that loomed in front of me. As we ascended a long, steep hill of 2.5 miles to reach the UC-Santa Cruz campus, it became apparent that this college looked quite different from the traditional East Coast universities. There weren't Gothic architecture or red brick buildings, separated by grassy quads. Instead, it was full of stucco roofs, glass buildings, and woods containing the legendary redwood trees I had only ever seen in pictures. John Steinbeck once observed, "The redwoods, once seen, leave a mark or create a vision that stays with you always. From them comes silence and awe." I was mesmerized when I took in those gargantuan trees for the first time.

The staff apartments were on the edge of campus, and as we climbed up the rickety staircase to what appeared to be a bungalow, I looked at the vast forest around me. My inner runner jumped for joy, as I realized that my backyard connected with a series of running trails that became the site of some of the most memorable runs of my life.

Prior to my arrival, I had emailed the 34 teachers I was going to be supervising to introduce myself in the hopes of making a good first impression. I provided some autobiographical information to highlight my experiences and to demonstrate that although I was a new dean, I was prepared for the added responsibilities of the position. I invited them to write back to me with their own introductions. Many of the high school teachers and college professors I would be supervising had more than twenty years of teaching experience. When the faculty met me for the first time, their startled expressions revealed that they weren't expecting that their new supervisor had just become old enough to rent a car.

After dinner, even though it felt like 10 p.m. to my jet-lagged body, I decided to go for a birthday run - something I had established as a new tradition a few years before. Given that I was directionally challenged, I thought this would be a good way to learn how to navigate around campus. As I happily trotted around, I caught a gorgeous sunset as I reached a cliff overlooking Santa Cruz and Monterey Bay. *I can't believe this is my home for the summer.* When I started to make my way back, I realized I was completely lost.

Even in a brand-new location, I foolishly believed that I could figure out the right path back. I knew the name of the building I was staying in, but was completely disoriented as dusk fell. I kept trying different parts of campus, hoping to finally stumble upon my living quarters. I started to panic. Nothing looked familiar. I did not own a smartphone: I couldn't pull up Google Maps and navigate my way back. Although I had my cell phone on me, I didn't really think I'd make a good impression if I called my boss to tell him that I was lost less than four hours after I'd arrived. The sky grew dark and there were no cars or pedestrians around. An hour later, a public safety van drove by, which I frantically hailed down. I explained to the officer that I was here for the summer, that it was my first day on campus, and that I was lost. Thankfully, he gave me a ride home. I quietly tiptoed up the stairs, hoping that none of my staff saw that I got escorted home like a lost kid at the mall. They already knew how young I was - I did not want them to think I was clueless as well. With these worries rattling around in my head and the adrenaline still pumping from the night's misadventure, it took hours for me to finally fall asleep. But I never got lost in Santa Cruz again.

***

That first week was challenging. At CTY, we used college spaces such as classrooms and residence halls as our miniature campus. Each summer, the administration arrives a week early to unpack our supplies from a storage unit and set up a pop-up program that is ready to welcome 250 children in seven days. As I coordinated lunch schedules, fire drills, and the opening ceremonies for Student Arrival Day, I was bombarded with classroom and supply requests from the teachers. When the university informed us that we only had limited laptops and projectors for the teachers to use, they were understandably frustrated. I feared that the teachers thought that I was inept. There were 34 of them, and I felt outnumbered. I needed to demonstrate that I was there to support the teachers, and that they could trust me to effectively lead the department.

I called for an impromptu faculty meeting in an effort to clear the air. As they trickled in, I tried to read their faces: some of which were full of frustration. I took several deep breaths to ensure that my voice and knees wouldn't shake as I spoke,

"I'm going to be honest: these first few days have been bumpy. You came into the summer with preconceived expectations, and due to circumstances beyond my control, you've been understandably disappointed with these issues. I regret that this has happened. But those are empty words. It is my goal to prevent these kinds of problems from cropping up again. I want to tell you how we as a team can move forward."

I then gave them a list of concrete steps I was going to take to improve the situation. Additionally, I described specific ways in which I hoped their feedback would shape our experience together and enable us to function as a cohesive team. I breathed a sigh of relief once the meeting was over. What surprised me was that afterwards, a few teachers approached me to thank me for handling an admittedly difficult meeting gracefully. The veteran teachers, amid half-smiles and eye rolls, informed me that the previous dean was a self-involved blowhard who never showed such vulnerability. The meeting ultimately righted the ship and gave me more credibility with the faculty. Not only did it help me become a better leader and an administrator, but I then took the lessons from this experience back to D.C.

***

Coming off my PR in Boston, I thought I was in good shape. But running in Santa Cruz highlighted the areas of improvement I needed to address. A five-mile run of the perimeter of campus had an elevation gain of 600 feet. There were a few occasions in the first couple weeks of running in Santa Cruz that I had to slow down to walk to catch my breath. The hills literally went on for miles on end and I felt my chest tighten - bringing me back to when I first started to run. I hadn't had to take a walking break in years! My apartment was at the top of the campus, so, whenever I went out and down the hill for a run, I always had to conserve enough energy to ensure that I made it back to the top at the end of the run.

***

July 10, 2011

Although my friends in D.C. have been sweating it out in the heat and humidity, it was foggy and 49 degrees this morning when I went out for my run. I was happy to don one of my long-sleeve Boston shirts with shorts: an outfit that I usually couldn't wear until late October. It's as if I've moved into an Olympic training camp. I have miles of trails at my disposal, a beautiful gym facility, an outdoor pool that I use for afternoon laps, and a hilly terrain that continues to callous and strengthen my muscles. This is easily the most beautiful place I've ever trained in: I love running amid the redwoods that stretch taller than the eye can see.

Today's run called for 11 miles with 10 x 90 second bursts of speed. The speed segments, even the ones uphill, didn't go beyond my aerobic threshold, like they had for my first few weeks in Santa Cruz. Instead, my legs were motoring and I was able to go with the flow. I had about two miles remaining, with a 600-foot climb to get to the top of campus, when I arrived at a red light. I was waiting for the light to change, and there was a cyclist on the opposite side of the road. I said to her, "I don't know how you manage to bike up these steep hills."

She responded, "Well, I am also a runner, and this is hard. Which way are you going?"

I pointed eastward, and she asked if we wanted to do the climb together. Inside my head, I thought, "What?! I can't run alongside a cyclist! This is going to be crazy!" But I responded with a resounding "Yes!"

United in our quest, we climbed our way up, happily chatting along the way. I felt like running through quicksand: the ascent was steep to begin with, I was trying to keep up a conversation, and I was running alongside someone who was moving on wheels.

As she gained speed, she cheered me on, "You're doing great, this is incredible!" Although I was tired, I finished feeling exhilarated. It was an unexpected way to finish the run, but completely worth it!

***

As administrators of a youth program, we constantly assured parents that their kids will be safe in our care. But on July 22, 2011, as I checked the news before heading into the office, I was horrified to learn that as kids played in an open field at a youth camp in Norway, a mass shooting brought utter devastation to a place that sought to embrace inclusivity and friendship. On the small island of Utøya, a man disguised as a police officer, shot and killed 69 people, mostly children. It was an unthinkable nightmare that brought my greatest fear to life. Ever since the Columbine shooting in 1999, which ushered in a new era of school shootings that were widely covered in the media, gun violence terrified me. As a teenager, I dreaded when we practiced lock-down drills because they made me imagine the worst-case scenario. Now as an adult, my fear was that I'd be unable to keep my students safe.

Reading the news coverage about such an atrocity at a summer camp took my breath away. Many of the kids who were murdered were 14 and 15 years old: the same age as our CTY students. Monica Bøsei, the camp director, approached the shooter in an attempt to protect the children, and was killed immediately. As someone with a tendency to imagine the worst-case scenario, it seemed too easy to envision such an atrocity occurring at CTY.

A day after the tragedy, the afternoon activity in Santa Cruz was an all-site Frisbee tournament on the lower east field of campus. The sounds of happy children playing, laughing, having carefree fun, was too much for me to handle, causing tears to roll down my face. I couldn't stop thinking about all of those children. Our kids, who couldn't see my reddened eyes behind my sunglasses, had no idea of what happened to their counterparts overseas. The juxtaposition of the two different camp experiences was overwhelming. I could only focus on protecting our children and ensuring that their summers were memorable for all the right reasons.

***

As the summer progressed, the faculty began to seek out

my guidance and look to me as a trusted colleague. The problems they brought to me varied: one was a brand-new teacher who struggled with classroom management, another looked for advice on how to work with students whose primary language was not English. Each time, my instructors sat on the large couch in my office. As we started to brainstorm, I could see their shoulders start to relax as we worked collaboratively to think through possible solutions. When one of the most widely-respected and adored instructors was leaving my office, she paused for a moment, "I'm glad I came in to see you. I feel so much better." That seal of approval made the growing pains of adjusting to the new position worthwhile.

***

August 13, 2011

It's 5 a.m., and I am at the Hartsfield-Jackson Atlanta International Airport, waiting for my last plane to complete my journey home. Even though I'm jet-lagged from this red-eye flight, I don't think I'll be able to fall asleep until I'm back in my own bed. After all of the highs and lows of the summer, I can't believe my CTY Santa Cruz experience has come to an end. Although I initially started off the summer staring at the calendar and wondering how I would get through the program, I'm leaving California feeling content. The kids had a wonderful time, stayed safe, and learned a lot. The staff did a great job, and I enjoyed working with them. Even though things felt rocky at the start, I managed to solve many of the problems and helped others grow during that process.

I took a leap of faith by stepping outside of my comfort zone and moving across the country for the summer. I had worked at the Saratoga site for five years, and while the thought of going elsewhere initially was hard to grasp, it was absolutely the right decision. It was similar to the leap of faith I took before the Boston Marathon. Again, I changed my plan, and while it seemed difficult at first, it yielded tremendous results.

Even though my responsibilities and workload had increased exponentially this summer, I loved this job and want to continue working with gifted students.

Chapter 8: Keep Showing Up

"Some days it just flows and I feel like I'm born to do this, other days it feels like I'm trudging through hell. Every day I make the choice to show up and see what I've got, and to try and be better. My advice: Keep showing up."
– Desiree Linden, 2018 Boston Marathon Champion

My Ph.D. comps were coming up at the end of October. I looked ahead to the Ph.D. exams with the same thrill I felt whenever Sarah sent me a hard training cycle. More than my master's lists, these reading lists were more tailored to my own research interests (no longer medieval witchcraft, but Christian devotion and practices of piety) in early medieval, early modern, and late medieval history. My doctoral reading lists doubled in size from my master's exams: totaling over 120 books. Although it was a tall order, I couldn't imagine a more enjoyable academic task than to spend weeks on end reading.

Each morning, I went out for a run, showed while the coffee brewed, and then read a book each day. I worked to commit each book to memory: its arguments, its sources, and it contributed to the larger field of medieval history. To do that, I created a huge stack of flashcards with the most salient information from each book. Whenever I went home to visit, my mom sat on the couch and quizzed me for hours. This was the same thing she did with vocabulary flashcards when I was studying for the SATs a decade before. She, along with my dad, continued to play a supportive and engaged role in my education.

Despite all of my studying, my nerves still got the best of me. A few weeks before the exam, I broke out into hives all over my arms and legs. I was completely in denial that this was stress-induced. Julie and I had recently moved into a new apartment, and I thought the hives were a reaction to the change in water. At every red light on my walk to school, I bent over to itch my legs. It was so hot in D.C., and the hives were visible anytime I wore a skirt. In class, I'd cross my legs, so that no one could see the reddened lumps all over the lower half of my body. There was a blatant physical reaction to my stress, yet I dismissed it. Instead, I focused on maintaining the rigorous pace required to keep up with my reading.

***

As I read *So Great a Light, So Great a Smoke: The Beguine Heretics of Languedoc* by Louisa Burnham in the middle of September, the word "indefatigable" appeared several times to discuss the relentless attitude of this particular religious movement in the late Middle Ages. The beguines were groups of women who lived in semi-monastic communities and stressed imitation of Christ's life through voluntary poverty, care of the poor and sick, and religious devotion. Even after I finished the book, I kept thinking about that word and its significance.

Runners are often called on to be indefatigable. We practice and practice running, doing long runs, tempo runs, intervals that get faster and faster with each subsequent lap, in the hopes that even as the hours and miles pass, we will not tire. We seek to find the perfect balance in challenging ourselves and improving our threshold. At the same time, we don't allow ourselves to burn out from the intensity. It is not easy.

In a similar manner, I sought to be indefatigable in my comps preparation. As much as I love reading, I also found it challenging to keep my mind attuned to the subtle differences in books on the same subject and retain the arguments of each piece of scholarship. It was as if I created an entire filing system in my brain, and the cabinets were full.

This is a sample of what a typical week looked like, in terms of both running and studying:

Monday September 12th

30 minutes on the elliptical, weights, strength, core
Sisters and Brothers of the Common Life: The Devotio Moderna and the World of the Later Middle Ages by John Van Engen

Tuesday September 13th

2.5-mile warm-up; 6 x 150-meter strides; 6x 1200 meters; start at 5:12 and cut down 3-5 seconds per interval; 400-meter jog between each interval; 2.5-mile cool-down. Total: 11.25 miles
The Laity in the Middle Ages: Religious Beliefs and Devotional Practice by André Vauchez

Wednesday September 14th

30 minutes on bike, weights, strength, core
start *Possible Lives: Authors and Saints in Renaissance Italy* by Alison Frazier

Thursday September 15th

8 miles easy
finish *Possible Lives: Authors and Saints in Renaissance Italy*

Friday September 16th

weights, strength, core
Literacy in Lombard Italy c. 568-774 by Nicholas Everett

Saturday, September 17th

2-mile warm-up; 6-mile tempo, 2-mile cool-down. Total: 10 miles
The Last Days of the Renaissance: And the March to Modernity by Theodore K. Rabb
So Great a Light, So Great a Smoke: The Beguine Heretics of Languedoc by Louisa Burnham

Sunday, September 18th

15.6 miles easy a.m., 3.4 miles easy p.m.
Images of the Educational Traveler in Early Modern England by Sara Douglass
start *Corpus Christi: The Eucharist in Late Medieval Culture* by Miri Rubin

Weekly Totals: 48 miles, 3 hours cross-training, 7 books

The training, both mental and physical, proved to be exhausting: and made me wonder if I really had what it took to be truly indefatigable. On my runs, my mind wandered as I thought about comps, but lacked real focus. I was surprised to soon discover that another athletic endeavor could also help me review for my exams.

***

By 2011, I had been swimming as a form of cross-training for two years, and finally started to feel comfortable in the water. Although my form was not graceful, I no longer looked like I was drowning as I completed my laps. My mind couldn't fully shut off underwater as it did during my runs. As I swam, I counted up the laps in 25-yard increments: 25, 50, 75, etc. I found it hard to zone out. If I lost track of my laps, there was no way to figure out exactly how far I'd swum. As I counted my reps, I came to notice that the numbers, such as "1225," "1350," sounded not like yard markers, but historical dates on a timeline. I renamed my 2,000-yard swim "The Swim to Modernity." In addition to knowing the content and significance of the books that appeared on my comps exams, I needed to have a good handle on the relevant chronology. This focused swim allowed me to review what has happened in 25-year increments and ensured that my lap counting remained accurate.

I loved getting in the pool for my nerdy workout: my body felt relaxed as I immersed myself underwater. As I went up and down the lane, I silently rattled off key dates that corresponded with the cumulative yardage: "426-Augustine's *City of God*, 476-Deposition of Romulus Augustulus, 511-death of Clovis, 540-*Rule of St. Benedict*, 751-beginning of the Carolingian Empire, 813-Synod of Mainz, 1076-Investiture Controversy, 1215-Fourth Lateran Council." On some days, I used the Swim to Modernity to sort through some of the key historiographical debates, "Ethnogenesis, barbarian identity, role of the laity in Christian burial practices, use of hagiography and the development of liturgical traditions, functions of Renaissance education." The workout helped identify the gaps of missing information and made the 45 minutes spent underwater go by quickly.

***

Two days before comps, I met Sarah on the track for a race simulation 5k. The rationale behind the race simulation was to see how hard I could run when someone else was managing the pace. As we laced up our sneakers, Sarah instructed, "Don't wear a watch. I'll take care of the pacing: tuck in behind me. We will be aggressive in the beginning, ease up slightly midway, and then push at the end." Sarah also said she was going to be interested to see what my effort looked like in person. Although I always emailed her the timed results of my track workouts, she didn't typically see me in action. Moreover, I had never raced a 5k on the track before. Regardless of my final time, I knew it would be a unique and challenging experience.

Because there was a field hockey game taking place on the inner field, we moved out to lane 5 of the track. From the very first lap, I felt tired. Part of it was comps fatigue, but it felt hard to run at break-neck speed. Sarah yelled out "6:30" for the first mile. I did not think I could do that again two more times. The middle section was really hard - Sarah was remained yards in front of me, and I could not catch her for the life of me. She kept yelling out, "Come on, come on!" My legs felt like lead and I couldn't respond to her call to pick up the pace.

"I am really blowing this and now I'm wasting Sarah's time. Ugh." I thought to myself. With a mile to go, two of our friends showed up to watch the field hockey game and cheered for me as I passed them. It was a surreal experience. While the stands were filled with people watching another game, they also tuned into what was happening on the track as Sarah and my friends cheered me on.

Sarah put two fingers up to mark that we had two laps left, then motioned for me to pick up the pace. But the lactic acid had built up too much in my legs to let me accelerate. Then, with one lap to go, I was able to get a little closer to Sarah. I tried to inch closer and closer, as my friends cheered me through the home stretch. I finished and stumbled off the track. I felt the taste of blood in the back of my throat – a clear sign I had run beyond my aerobic threshold.

Sarah, looking fresh, asked how I felt. "That was one of my hardest runs ever!" I exclaimed, between gasps for air. Looking at her watch, she replied, "Well, it should've felt hard. You ran 19:57!"

I was stunned. I figured I had run much slower. Sarah thought that the time equated to about 20:15 on the road, which was my fastest time ever. As I caught my breath, Sarah said, "This is what a 5k should feel like: really uncomfortable the whole time. Since you're coming from a marathon background, you've learned how to preserve your energy, and that needs to go out the window for shorter distances. As you move down to these faster races, you'll need to be more aggressive from the gun and be prepared to deal with an uncomfortable pace for the entire race." That advice shaped my running for years to come.

***

When I trained for my big races, I always tried to take it easy during the taper, with the goal of emerging on race day feeling rested and ready to go. But the first day of comps was the day after the simulator 5k, and I woke up feeling rundown. The combination of lack of quality sleep and the hard workout led to a chest cold and laryngitis.

The written exam was completed in a professor's office on a Word document without access to the Internet. Thankfully, it was a typed exam, because as my friend Pam once commented, "You know, for such a nice person, your handwriting is atrocious." I breathed a sigh of relief as I looked at the essay prompts: all seemed manageable. I set to work: first outlining my essays, and then typing away rapidly. The four hours went by quickly. I made it through Day 1.

With Day 2 right around the corner, all I could do was clear my head in the afternoon, and then review my notes briefly that evening. I went to bed full of anticipation: I spent more time and energy preparing for Day 2. I felt a knot tightening in my stomach as I walked in the exam room. Thankfully, I was working in a private office, as I couldn't stop coughing.

I was pleased with the essays I chose to answer on Day 2. The ideas quickly spilled out of my head and I even used footnotes to supplement my main points. We were given a choice of which questions to write about, although the omitted questions are fair game on the day of the oral exam. Relieved to have made it over the hurdle of the written portion, I went home, took some NyQuil, and crawled into bed. I slept for nine hours, which was much more than the previous few nights of sleep combined. Even though I still had the orals, I had a few days to gear up and get ready for them, which included getting my voice back.

The oral exam was a one-hour grilling session from the four professors on my committee. Virtually anything was fair game: they could ask me to clarify things from the written exam, to give verbal answers to the questions that I chose to omit, as well as broader topics about the field. The oral exam terrified me. At least in the written exam, I could pause and think through things. A verbal test required almost instantaneous, thought-out responses. I had studied with these professors for three years and wanted to show that I had matured in terms of my analysis and response. I tossed and turned all night as I fretted about the exam.

The morning of my orals, I went on a 3-mile run, trying to calm my nerves. As I ran around the campus perimeter, the same route that I had run hundreds of miles on while becoming a marathon runner, I reminded myself that I was well-prepared and ready. I kept repeating to myself, "You are finally becoming the person you wanted to be."

I got dressed in one of my most professional academic outfits: pencil skirt, blue blouse, and grey blazer. It was my attempt to look more like a professor, rather than someone who was often confused for an undergrad. I sat at the Starbucks on campus before the exam, reviewing my notes and trying to breathe. As I sipped my coffee, Dr. Paxton, one of my professors, came up to me: "There's no need to be terrified, your written exams were fine, this will be a breeze." While I appreciated her support and positivity, I still didn't think it would be that easy.

Each professor had 15 minutes to ask a series of complex questions. Dr. Jansen even read back to me the last sentence of one of my written responses and asked me to justify that claim. I tensed up. While I was writing the exam, I had hastily made a claim about the complex relationship between masculinity and religion in the late Middle Ages that was merely meant to provide a flourishing conclusion to my essay. Now, Dr. Jansen asked for evidence to back it up. Scrambling for an answer, I spoke about St. Francis of Assisi and Thomas Aquinas, while citing some of the gender theory texts that Dr. Jansen had assigned back in my first semester.

It was going well, but it was definitely not a breeze, as Dr. Paxton predicted. Although I had managed to answer most of the questions quickly, I asked for a moment to pause and collect my thoughts to answer one particularly difficult question on early Christian burial practices. After about 30 seconds of awkward silence, Dr. Sherman mused to the other professors, "What exactly defines early Christianity?" This sparked a flurry of discussion amongst my professors. As intimidated as I was by them, I shot them a look that said, "I need to concentrate – please be quiet!" At first, they seemed taken aback, then they immediately apologized. The subsequent silence enabled me to come up with my answer.

After getting through that challenging question, they also asked me to tie the four fields together (which, chronologically spanned the years 300-1800) - not an easy task. Finally, they sent me into the hall. It was time for them to vote on whether I passed or not.

As I sat outside to wait for their verdict, the knot in my stomach emerged again while they deliberated. Finally, the door opened, and Dr. Jansen announced, "Congratulations, you passed!"

All of my professors congratulated me, and we walked out chatting about the exam. They teased me about how I glared at them when they interrupted my thought process, "Vanessa, we've never seen you look that irritated!" At the encouragement of Dr. Jansen, I even had a celebratory glass of wine with Wes and Julie at lunch. That evening, my friends from the history department went out to Colonel Brooks, our favorite neighborhood pub. That night, tipsy and exhausted, I slept for almost 12 hours straight. It felt like such sweet bliss to finally sleep without thinking about (or dreaming of) exams.

Three days after comps, the stress hives finally disappeared from my legs, more than six weeks after they first emerged. My mental stress had manifested into physical symptoms. But, like other moments in my life when I was confronted with anxiety, I attributed my stress to the situation, and was reluctant to think that this was a lifelong problem. Instead, I turned my eyes forward to the next chapter in my graduate career.

Chapter 9: Not in Vain

"Recognize your victories."
– Joan Benoit Samuelson, 1984 Olympic Marathon Champion

Although I knew that I wanted to write my dissertation on a topic within the field of late medieval religious history, the specific area remained unclear after my comprehensive exams. In one of our regular meetings, Dr. Jansen suggested that I read Miri Rubin's *Mother of God: A History of the Virgin Mary*, "Vanessa, you should consider writing about the Virgin Mary. This book will give you a lot to think about as you discern a possible topic." As I read, I was fascinated to read about all of the intricate culture and devotional practices that emerged in the Middle Ages that were all focused on venerating the Blessed Virgin Mary. As a Catholic, Mary had always played a role in my faith: I found her to be a comforting person to turn to in moments of doubt and hesitation. And as a historian, I thought it would be intriguing to research the ways in which the most influential woman in Western religion shaped medieval Christian culture.

"Just read, Vanessa. Don't search for a topic – let the sources speak to you," Dr. Jansen advised, "Too many people try to force a topic from the reading. Keep an open mind, and eventually, you'll land on something that you know you'll want to write about for years on end." To cultivate a regular writing habit, I kept a dissertation diary that I filled with notes and questions that emerged from my reading.

***

That January, I attended a department workshop to learn more about the next benchmark in my Ph.D. program: the dissertation proposal. The proposal was the document I had to get approved by Dr. Jansen, my committee, the history department, and eventually, the School of Arts and Sciences. The workshop freaked me out a bit - it was overwhelming to think about how I would plan out my dissertation.

Feeling motivated from the workshop, Wes, Julie, and I opted to stay on campus and get some work done. We ended up working in the TA office until 10 p.m. – pretty late for a Friday night. I was able to focus and stay on task knowing that my friends were also writing. It snowed all evening, which made for a pretty view while we worked.

When I walked home at the end of the night, my feet crunched in the freshly-fallen snow as I tried to digest the events of the day. I was a little overwhelmed from the workshop, and seeking some inspiration, I plugged in my ear buds and played "Find Your Grail" from the musical *Spamalot*, a song that talks about conquering your fears,

Life is really up to you,
You must choose what to pursue,
Set your mind on what you find,
And there's nothing you can't do.

Cheesy as it may be, the song uplifted me, and offered a reminder that all big dreams are accompanied with some fear and doubt.

***

In the Spring 2012 semester, I was fortunate to land the opportunity to teach at Mount St. Mary's University, a Catholic liberal arts college in Emmitsburg, Maryland. Their history department asked the CUA history department to recommend some doctoral students to teach a Renaissance survey course. Renaissance history was one of my minor fields for comps, and I was thrilled to get the chance to take the lead role in a class for the first time.

Over the Christmas break, I prepped for class. I was eager to assign books that had excited me about this historical era, including a couple that I first read at Holy Cross. I wanted to make sure that my students would be as excited about the historical texts they'd study as I was nearly a decade before.

That Christmas, my parents had given me a series of gifts to help me transition from grad student to adjunct professor. My mom gave me a few new snazzy outfits and a stylish black bag to carry all of my teaching materials. My dad got me something that would be equally, if not more, essential: a Garmin GPS.

Mount St. Mary's University is 70 miles from D.C, and at a minimum, it took an hour and a half to make the trip each way. My parents were kind enough to loan me one of their cars for the semester, as they recognized that I was given a great opportunity to teach at a relatively young age. But they were taking a big risk in doing this: I was terrified of driving. Before that semester, the most I had ever driven in a single stretch was about twenty miles. I had relatively little experience driving in the city or the highway: both key elements of this commute. When I was a teenager, my dad was incredibly patient when it came to my driving and taught me how to parallel park in preparation for my road test.

Almost a decade later, he drove with me from Rochester to D.C., with plans to fly back the following day after leaving the car with me. We stopped to walk around Mount St. Mary's, and then he said, "Okay, Vanessa, it's your turn to take the wheel." I was a mess as soon as we pulled out of campus: I had trouble merging and switching lanes. People honked at me, and on more than one occasion, I nearly sideswiped a car. We both yelled and cursed at each other throughout the 90-minute trip. At last, we pulled into church to attend Sunday Mass. Apparently not feeling the presence of the Holy Spirit just yet, I slammed the car door in frustration, causing other church-goers to stop and stare. My dad and I could barely speak to each other as we bowed our heads reverently as we entered church. After we walked out of Mass, my dad said, "You have to get back out there. You need more practice." Despite my protests, we headed back to the car for another round of city driving lessons. This second iteration was barely an improvement on the afternoon drive: no amount of praying during (or after) Mass had helped me.

Later that night, while I was unpacking the car, my dad

confessed to my roommate Julie, "Oh God, I hope the car and Vanessa make it through the semester in one piece." He flew home the following day: both of us were uncertain how things would pan out.

I was more nervous about the six hours I'd spend each week in the grey Chevy Aveo, compared to the hours of lecturing I'd do in front of my students. After my first class, which included a few near-misses with other cars, I was so rattled that I couldn't stop babbling about the trek to Julie. Her eyes widened as I continued to ramble. "Vanessa, I think you need a glass of wine to unwind - you're way too tense," she said gently, trying to find some way to calm me down. Opening the fridge, I grabbed a bottle of pinot grigio and poured myself a generous glass. After a few sips, I began to decompress, but gripped the glass with the same firmness that I had as I clutched the steering wheel an hour before. At the end of each day as I pulled into our apartment complex, I mentally checked off how many trips to Emmitsburg I had left for the semester. Unwinding with a glass of wine became my ritual to relax and breathe a sigh of relief that another day of driving on the Beltway was over.

I adapted to teaching much quicker: I enjoyed putting together lectures on the Bubonic Plague, the Reformation, and the French Revolution. After spending most of the day reading for my dissertation, I left Washington at 3 p.m. On the scenic drive, I passed farmhouses and fields filled with cows grazing, I listened to classical music and tried my best to not irritate other drivers on I-270. I taught at 5 p.m., and then held office hours immediately after. In the small office that I shared with several other adjuncts, I graded papers, responded to emails, and met with students. Around 7:30, I drove back, arriving home around 9 p.m., fried from the combination of the long day and harrowing commute.

Aside from the driving, it was a good first experience teaching. More importantly, it proved to my own department at CUA that I was ready to teach at my home university.

***

During my first year at CUA, my friend Kate Bush, an advanced doctoral student, taught Junior Seminar, one of the required courses for the history major. Curious how she got the position, I asked her about the application process, thinking that it would be good for me to know down the road. "Oh, they asked me to teach it," Kate replied, matter-of-factly. *Really? Wow, she must be really good if our professors sought her out.*

One morning before class, I received an email from our department chair, Dr. Muller,

Vanessa,

I'd like to talk to you about whether you might be interested in teaching HIST 387 (Junior Seminar) during the fall semester.

Dr. Muller

This invitation came less than two years after I sat in Dr. Muller's office, wondering if I had any future at CUA. While explaining the premise of the class, Dr. Muller said, "the department is particularly excited to have you teach this course, Vanessa." *Really?*

Dr. Muller then proceeded to discuss the logistics of teaching the class. My mind went into overdrive – this time, on a happy occasion. I was thrilled. I had spent a good chunk of my grad experience looking up to the grad students like Kate and Wes who really seemed to have it all together. This offer proved that the faculty believed that I could fully take the reins of a class. It was a great moment in my young career.

***

My big running goal for Spring 2012 was to break 20 minutes in the 5k: a big goal among amateur runners. Taking on this challenge both excited and terrified me. The track workouts Sarah had assembled for me were going well: all signs pointed to sub-20. Sarah even had me graduate from regular sneakers to racing flats. These racing shoes barely weighed six ounces and were designed to help me become a more efficient runner. The Saucony Endorphin 2 shoes were sleek, fluorescent yellow, and I felt lightning-quick as soon as I slipped them on. It was game time.

My goal race was the Scope It Out 5k on Pennsylvania Avenue: one of the fastest courses in D.C. This was the place to run hard and leave nothing on the line. I was worried about how tough it was going to feel: Sarah told me to ignore the pain and gut it out.

On race morning, it was 50 degrees, cool, and with a touch of light rain. Compared to the freezing rain that came earlier in the week, this was heavenly! I completed my warm up on the course, which gave me a good idea what the first and last mile looked like - flat and straight.

Sarah recommended to go out hard and try to bank some time early on in the race. Although that tactic would be ill-advised in a marathon, going out hard is feasible in a shorter race. I got through the first mile in 6:15 and felt really solid. I now had 10 extra seconds in the bank. There were a couple of women who were ahead of me. Although I wasn't planning on making a move until later in the race, I realized that they were slowing down and passed them decisively. A woman in pink passed me, but I passed her right back a hundred yards later. We then hit mile 2 in 12:40, which meant that I had slowed to 6:26. Although that was my goal race pace and I had 10 seconds "in the bank," I did not want to finish in 20:01. The final mile was all about pushing hard. The woman in pink passed me again, and I let her go. Although I was out there to race against other people, more than anything, I was racing against the clock.

Starting at about 15:00, I kept checking my watch every few hundred meters. Although I was tired, I was also fired up about breaking 20 minutes and knew that nothing, even fatigue, could slow me down. The woman in pink reappeared in front of me with about 800 meters to go. I could hear her breathing heavily: a sign her energy was waning. I passed her with confidence at the 3-mile mark - 19:02. All I needed to do was kick hard down as I headed down Pennsylvania Avenue. I had the biggest smile on my face as they announced, "Here comes Vanessa Taylor, one of our top female finishers!"

I crossed the line in 19:39 (6:20 pace) and staggered to a

stop. Trying to catch my breath, I was doubled over with my hands on my knees. The expression on my face was one of disbelief and joy, and I knew that I would remember this feeling for a long time. Breaking 20 minutes was a huge mental and physical barrier, and standing on the other side of it felt absolutely tremendous. Cracking open some champagne that night to celebrate, I was excited for what it signaled for my running in the future.

***

I had developed big aspirations: I wanted to run fast, earn my Ph.D. but I also wanted a supportive partner. It had been a few years since I broke up with Matthew, and I was finally ready to date. Although I prided myself on being self-sufficient and independent, I was looking for some extra support and for someone to want to share these experiences with me. After years of being single, I had finally found my own self-worth that was not tied up to having a boyfriend. The majority of my classmates were in serious relationships, and all of my best girlfriends were already married. Unlike in college, I didn't need a boyfriend to feel successful or validated. Nevertheless, I still longed for companionship. I did not have any experience dating casually, and upon several recommendations, I signed up for eHarmony on January 3, 2012. The process was overwhelming: the initial questionnaire took hours to complete. Within a day, my inbox was flooded with messages from local singles who wanted to meet me.

My first round of dates included a lot of odd matches. One was with a guy who thought women should only wear skirts and dresses - this came up while I was sitting across from him in the cafe wearing jeans. On a second date, one man gave me a necklace that said "You are special to me," which seemed to be more fitting for kids to give to their moms on Mother's Day. That necklace quickly found a home at Goodwill. Another date ended when we met up with his friends in a tattoo parlor in a basement in Bethesda. I was dressed in one of my fancy teaching outfits, complete with a pearl necklace, and should've worn a sign that said, "I don't belong here." After those mismatches, I turned off the notifications for a couple of weeks.

However, in early February, I started to exchange messages with a handsome lawyer named Pat, a member of the National Guard who had served in Iraq and now worked with veterans to help them receive disability compensation. Pat's profile made me laugh, "I have two black belts, one in taekwondo and one in Microsoft Office 2010 – I'm MS Excel-ent." I got a different vibe from Pat than I did from the other guys. After a few weeks of exchanging friendly emails, he finally asked if I wanted to meet in person.

Pat told me that he had never been to CUA before and suggested that we take a walk around campus and maybe grab coffee afterwards. For the middle of winter, February 18th was a beautiful sunny day with the temperature reaching almost 60 degrees. Although I tried to appear put together in my online profile, this wasn't the case in reality. I was running late, so late that I had painted my nails right before I walked out the door and was frantically blowing my hands to dry as I walked to meet Pat near the Brookland-CUA metro.

I wasn't the only one who was rushing around: Pat texted me to apologize for his delay. I sat on a bench, waiting nervously. *Take a deep breath, relax, and don't say anything ridiculous.* Reminding me of Tom Hanks at the end of *You've Got Mail* (one of my favorite movies), Pat came up the stairs off the metro, wearing a big smile on his face, his eyes bright with excitement.

Enjoying the gorgeous day, we strolled around campus. I pointed out all the key buildings: O'Connell Hall – the history department, Centennial Village – where I worked for two years, Seton Hall – the old residence for nuns that was my home as a master's student. He listened carefully, asking questions and gradually sharing information about himself. After our tour of CUA, we grabbed coffee, and continued our conversation there. When the date was over, we hugged goodbye, and Pat said he'd be in touch. *I hope I get to see him again – that was a nice first date.*

A few days later, Pat emailed me to ask me out again – this time to the National Zoo. As we checked out the pandas and giraffes, Pat told me that when he was studying for the bar exam, he house-sat for a family that had an English bulldog, and had such a wonderful time that he hoped to get one someday. As a dog-lover myself, I filed this anecdote away, along with all of the other tidbits we started to share with each other.

One weeknight, Pat suggested a picnic at the National Mall. Even though our department sponsored a talk I had to attend that afternoon, I happily listened to the guest speaker lecture on the queens of medieval Spain, knowing that I had a fun date to look forward to afterwards. Following our picnic, we walked around the mall, taking in the monuments: Washington Monument, the Lincoln Memorial, World War II, etc. Even though we both had lived in Washington for years, it was enjoyable to visit these landmarks together. We shared stories of the times we had previously visited these historic sites with our families and on school trips. The hours flew by: we didn't leave until nearly 10 p.m. (on a "school night!" – I thought to myself).

I found him attractive for many reasons, but not only because of his bright eyes and warm smile. It was clear that Pat respected me and celebrated my achievements with me. When I told him about the offer to teach Junior Seminar, his face lit up with genuine excitement. Matthew often felt jealous or threatened by my accomplishments. Pat, on the other hand, shared in the joy that came from any success I earned.

***

Whenever Pat talked about his childhood, he said how he grew up on a farm "in the middle of nowhere," which I always took to be an exaggeration. He talked about getting up at the crack of dawn as a child to feed the animals, and as he grew older, helping his father make hay in the summer for the horses. When it was time to meet his parents, I chose a purple silk skirt and a pair of black heels that I bought just for the occasion. When he picked me up, Pat kissed me, "You look really nice. They're going to love you." He never indicated that my outfit was inappropriate for dinner at his parents' home.

While we drove the 60 miles from Washington to the farm in rural Maryland, Pat told anecdotes about his childhood, which included a lot of farming terms that were completely unfamiliar to me. As we got closer to the house, the roads switched from asphalt to gravel, and then to dirt. We wound our way up the narrow roads, the car thudding on the uneven parts. At last, we pulled up to the picturesque farmhouse. I took a deep breath, and then stepped out of the car. Immediately, my brandnew heels sank into the grass, still soggy from the rainstorm the night before. "Oh no!" I cried out. Pat looked at me and laughed, "Don't worry about it." Grabbing Pat's arm, I inched my way to the house on my tiptoes, looking like a baby deer learning how to walk. I reached the porch, happy to return to steady ground.

Pat opened the door, and his parents warmly greeted us. His mother even helped me clean the mud from my shoes. Over dinner, Ann and Howie asked me stories about my interest in medieval history, and they showed me adorable pictures of Pat as a baby. As we cleared our plates, Pat said, "Why don't I give you a tour of the rest of the farm?"

The rest of? Their property seemed to go on for miles on end - how would we see it? Once again, I ungainly walked outside, as Pat led me to a 4-wheeler. "Hop on!" he encouraged me. "Pat, I'm wearing a skirt, I can't hop on," I protested. "Just sit on my lap, and I'll hold onto you. No one will see you," he said. Looking to make sure that Pat's parents hadn't slipped out behind us, I ungracefully climbed on, clinging tightly to Pat.

Miss Manners (and my mom) would've had a stroke if she saw me with my legs spread open in my skirt as we drove through the fields. I was grateful that the horses couldn't talk or react to the sight of my bright pink underwear, now visible to anyone who saw us whizzing by. When we entered the house again, my hair, which I carefully styled just hours before, looked like it had gone through a wind tunnel. Ann asked, "Did you enjoy the tour?" I smiled sheepishly as I replied, "Yes, but I'm going to need a different outfit the next time I'm here."

***

After spending a semester reading medieval sources about the Virgin Mary, I started to observe some interesting patterns in these devotional sources. As a lifelong Catholic, I loved looking at images of the Virgin Mary while I was sitting in the pews during Mass. I typically envisioned her as the maiden who quaked at the sight of the angel Gabriel at the Annunciation, or the young mother looking over the infant Jesus in Nativity scenes. On the contrary, these miracle collections depicted Mary as a strong woman, and when combating forces of evil, her words and behavior could be described as vengeful.

For example, in his twelfth-century *Miracles of the Virgin Mary*, a monk named William of Malmesbury wrote that Mary beat the devil with a stick, "redoubling her blows and making them sharper with words, 'Take that, and go away. I warn you and order you not to harass my monk any more. If you dare to do so, you will suffer worse.'" I was flummoxed. This powerful depiction of Mary was in stark opposition to the obedient woman who said at the Annunciation, "Behold the handmaid of the Lord: be it done to me according to thy word." After reading this, I wrote in my notebook, "These stories, which demonstrate Mary not as a compassionate intercessor, but as a potent intermediary, can also show the emerging complexity of the medieval understanding of Mary." Perhaps this was enough of an insight to launch a new topic.

At the end of April, Dr. Sherman organized a workshop for students working on dissertation proposals. As I spoke about what I observed in the *miracula*, she asked "What does it mean when Mary speaks?" This question gave me a lot to think about as I started to move deeper into my research. I was confident this was *the* project that would be the ticket to my Ph.D.

***

At the end of May, I was home in Rochester visiting my parents for a few weeks. While they were at work, I worked on getting some writing in each day. One day, when looking for some secondary research material, I logged into a history dissertation database, and found a 2006 dissertation by a UC-Berkeley student named Kathleen A. Stewart: "Domina Misericordiae: Miracle Narratives and the Virgin Mary, 1130-1230." *Are you kidding me?*

My eyes welled up with tears as I started to read the introduction of this dissertation – finding this finished piece of research was a kick in the stomach. I had already written 20 pages of analysis on the topic, now apparently for naught.

Shutting my laptop, I went up to my childhood room, and flopped onto my bed to cry, like I had so many times as a young girl in the face of failure. A few hours later, my dad called to check in, and I answered the phone in tears. "What happened?" he asked, knowing that I had been excited about my summer work. I hastily explained my discovery.

I was frustrated that even though I was putting time into my research, I couldn't land on a topic. I was fried and dejected, and I needed to put my research aside and focus on something else.

I returned to California for another summer as the CTY academic dean. On the weekends when I had time off, I went to the UC-Santa Cruz library to read more about Marian miracle collections, in hopes of finding a new research angle. I also wrote to Dr. Jansen, explaining the situation and some of the new ideas I was bouncing around. I was hoping to give her a summer update filled with good news, not a roadblock. But she had advised students for years, and knew that there were often obstacles throughout the process, which was why she reminded me, "Your reading won't be in vain."

That became my mantra for the next phase of graduate school.

Chapter 10: The Proposal

"Dare to compete." – Billie Jean King, winner of 39 Grand Slam titles and winner over Bobby Riggs in the "Battle of the Sexes"

Before I headed back to D.C. to start the new semester, I went home to Rochester. I appreciated the opportunity to unwind and relax after a busy summer with CTY. While I was home, I also signed up to run a 5k with my parents. It was great to witness first-hand how much progress they made since they took up running.

Although my mom was always very healthy, she never considered herself athletic. After she saw me get into marathoning, my mom started off by running a couple of miles on the treadmill at the YMCA a few days a week. A few months after my debut marathon, she started to venture outside. In 2010, my mom ran her first 5k, and has since completed more than a dozen half marathons, running times that make friends my own age jealous. Mom quickly took to all of the things I loved about the sport: she'd call me up to talk about training, improving on her race time, and deciding what race to sign up for next. Her success in distance running, which did not happen until her early 50s, is a testament to the amazing things that the human body can learn how to do.

My dad, who was a collegiate swimmer and avid cyclist, also proudly stood at the finish line of all of my marathons. Knowing his natural competitiveness, especially since he watched my mom take to running relatively easily, it made sense that he too felt compelled to give running a go. Yet, for someone who said for years that running always gave him shin splints, my dad learned how to train slowly, and also started to enter 5ks.

Unlike my mom, who ran four days a week, my dad managed to get by on one or two runs a week. He maintained his endurance through his regular swims and bike rides on the Erie Canal with his friends. When Dad remarked to me and my mom, after the two of us had finished a ten-mile race, that he wanted to run one as well, we retorted, "You know, you actually have to run regularly!" Taking our words to heart, he eventually trained for and finished several half marathons: an impressive feat for someone who didn't take up running until his mid-fifties.

As I began to compete more frequently in shorter-distance races, I sometimes won my age group or finished in the top five overall. At the start of some races, having researched the top times from the previous year, I'd think to myself, "Maybe if I have a great day, I could win this race." As I stood on the starting line, I'd glance around to assess whether my competitors looked "fast enough" to beat me. On several occasions, I ran with the lead pack, and the excitement built in my head: "Maybe this will finally happen this time." But a woman (or sometimes two or three) who had another gear left in the final stretch pulled away, leaving me to shelve my hope of winning for another day.

My parents and I spent the morning getting ready for the 5k: pinning our bib numbers onto our shirts, stretching, and warming up. I wished them luck and then headed to the front of the pack. Once again, I sized up the other women, trying to get a sense of who would be my fellow competitors. As I ran out with the lead pack of women, even though the pace felt hard, I knew I had another gear in me. Three women ran alongside me: none of us eager to take the pace out hard too early. I had learned how to read the body language of other runners. I could tell who was tired based on sagging shoulders or ragged breathing. One woman's breaths became increasingly labored after the first mile - I took it as a sign that I'd be able to pass her soon.

At the turnaround mark, I surged ahead, eager to put some distance between me and the other women. None of them attempted to match my pace, and I had opened up a fifty-yard lead. Going down the back stretch, I could see that as long as I maintained this pace, I could win the race. A few spectators started to clap and cheer, "First woman!" as I ran by. "I hope I can keep this up," I thought to myself, "Because this feels awesome." I felt focused and dialed in.

Wanting to protect first place, I sped up, thinking I should try to keep a large gap between me and the woman in second place. I peeked back a couple of times to make sure no one was going to blow by me. This is not a tactical move, as it can let your competition know you're feeling antsy or tired. No one was in sight. I saw the finish line in the distance, and my excitement grew as winning became closer in my grasp. With ten yards to go, two race officials held out a large finish tape, at which point I lifted my hands in the air in victory, yelling out a huge "YEAH!"

In my marathons and other races, I had crossed the finish line filled with a sense of pride and accomplishment. Personal bests were always exciting - they signaled my best performances ever. But winning a race was a different kind of achievement. On that day, I was the fastest woman out of 300 women. The $200 cash prize was an added bonus, on top of telling each of my parents, as they finished the race a few minutes back, that I had won. That sense of satisfaction fueled me to train harder, and to remember that feeling of triumph during moments of grad school when my confidence in my research wavered.

***

Back in D.C. for the fall semester, I taught Junior Seminar for the first time and enjoyed getting to know my class. Each week, we gathered to discuss one book and its contributions to historical research. Although it was challenging to get the students to talk and carry a two-hour conversation in the beginning, we eventually settled into a rhythm. It was fun to see the different areas of a study that fascinated my students, and I felt proud as I watched their writing improve through the semester.

Although it would be years before I'd finish my dissertation, I already started to think about possible career options. The natural progression after earning a Ph.D. in history is to pursue a tenure-track job at a university. The reality of the job market is that there are very few job openings, especially for medieval historians. When one of my more senior classmates graduated, she applied for the *six* tenure-track jobs that were open to medieval historians that year *in the country*. When the rejection notices started coming in, each letter noted that she was one of more than 200 applicants for the job. I loved teaching, and while I was improving as a student, I also recognized that the odds of me beating out over 200 applicants for a job were not in my favor.

In an effort to prepare us for the job market, the history department brought in alumni who had used their doctorates in different sectors: working for the government, consulting in the private sector, and for some, becoming an adjunct professor. Adjuncts are severely underpaid, they don't receive benefits, sometimes don't even get their own office, and are regarded by many as professors-adjacent. Adjuncts often teach beyond a normal course load to make even a fraction of what the tenured and tenure-track professors earn. They are treated as contingent faculty and their job status is never secure.

One of the panelists, a medievalist who studied under Dr. Jansen, said that she drove more than 100 miles each way to get to teach at three different universities. I was astonished. It was one thing for me to do that twice a week while teaching at Mount St. Mary's as a young graduate student: it was another to make that the sole basis of my livelihood as a middle-aged adult. I walked out of that workshop knowing that I wasn't going to pursue a tenure-track job, nor would I seek to cobble together a series of adjunct gigs that left me underpaid and overworked.

Although I loved teaching, I also knew that my own skill sets went beyond the classroom. All of the leadership work I had done as a CTY academic dean had positioned me for jobs in academic support. This meant I could serve as an academic advisor, run a tutoring center, lead a university's honors program, or other positions that blended leadership skills with classroom management. Not all academics like this kind of work, but I enjoyed it immensely. As I researched these jobs, I also learned that some of these positions included the opportunity to teach part-time. I could remain immersed in medieval history, while finding gainful employment in a field that valued some of my other interpersonal skills. I still envisioned a career at a university, but one that looked different from the paths my professors took.

***

On Friday December 14, 2012, I was in the middle of grading final papers at the Starbucks on campus. In need of a break from grading, I logged onto CNN.com to read the news. My heart sank when I read: "Breaking News: School Shooting in Connecticut." Within a few hours, it was reported that 6 educators and 20 first graders were murdered at Sandy Hook Elementary School. The people around me in the coffee shop must not have seen the news, as they casually breezed chatted with friends. My hand covered my mouth in shock as I read about how an assault rifle designed for war mowed down 6- and 7-year-old kids in less than 10 minutes. Most of the children were never even brought to the hospital because the damage from the multiple gunshot wounds was irreparable. I left campus in tears, unable to think about anything else.

The individual stories that emerged in the ensuing days made these victims seem more memorable, and their final moments continue to haunt me. Even almost a decade later, they still come to mind anytime the words "school shooting," "Newtown," or "Sandy Hook" are uttered, instantly transporting me back to that horrific day.

Dawn Hochsprung, the school principal who dressed up in funny costumes for school spirit days, heroically lunged at the shooter, sacrificing her life in an attempt to protect her students. Anne Marie Murphy, an aide to six-year-old Dylan Hockley, was found cradling Dylan in her arms, offering him love and protection until the bitter end. Jesse Lewis, at 6 years old, told his classmates to "run!" while the shooter reloaded. Those were his last words: many of Jesse's classmates were able to escape because of his heroic warning.

This particular massacre hit too close to home. My mom is an elementary school reading specialist, and my cousins Meryl and Rory were also in first grade at the time. It could've easily happened at their schools. The news coverage was relentless and heartbreaking. Relatives of the victims told newscasters that there were presents lovingly wrapped by parents that would never be open, and outfits intended for Christmas Day became the clothes for their burials. The season of Advent, a time of waiting, had suddenly turned into a season for mourning. At Christmas Eve Mass, tears streamed down my face as we listened to our children's choir sing "Silent Night." Their angelic voices sounded all the more precious against the backdrop of this catastrophe.

I went back to D.C. at New Year's, and tried to move past this tragedy, like most people had. I wrote to my government representatives about gun safety and mental health and donated to newly-formed grassroots movements such as Sandy Hook Promise and Moms Demand Action for Gun Sense in America. I hoped that taking tangible steps to make our country safer would help lessen the feelings of helplessness and hopelessness that consumed me.

But each morning, that rational thinking disappeared when I walked to the metro. My neighborhood on Capitol Hill was filled with children walking to school. Seeing these children, with their backpacks almost as big as them, and hearing their chirpy voices, as they kissed their parents goodbye, caused me to tear up nearly every day. They were living reminders of the Sandy Hook shooting. I despaired about the state of our country. How could I feel joy when others lost so much in this violent tragedy? How could I ever think about having children if they could die in such a horrific manner? I had no answers. When I returned to teaching for the spring semester, I carefully evaluated the exits, places for my students to hide, and how to shelter in place. I felt increasingly anxious about my own safety and that of my students. Moreover, I had trouble sleeping, as worst-case scenarios ran through my head late into the night.

The ongoing inability to sleep was making it more difficult for me to function as a grad student. I'd often feel too tired to work for more than a couple of hours in a row. It was the middle of March, and the insomnia continued. During one of our regular phone calls, my best friend Kathleen and I were chatting about her residency as a new dermatologist. She switched gears and asked how the dissertation was going. I unloaded on her how I hadn't had a good night's sleep for months and how helpless and scared I felt in the wake of the Newtown shooting. "Kathleen, what can I do?" I asked her, desperate for a solution. "I feel stuck, and I don't know how things are going to get better."

She proceeded cautiously, "Vanessa, I know that this has been a rough patch, but I also know that you've dealt with this kind of anxiety before. I can list off all of the times when you internalized all of your worries, and then shut down. That's no way to live. And you know I've dealt with this myself as well - it can be good to talk to a professional. They can help you get out of your head. They'll work with you and teach you strategies to cope. Think about it, okay? I hope you give it a chance. I care about you too much to see you hurting like this."

Heeding Kathleen's advice, I signed up for free counseling that was made available to students at CUA. I had never considered counseling before, mainly because I had deemed my worries to be "not significant enough" to merit professional help. But I couldn't continue to ignore the ways in which my constant worrying impacted my daily life. Once a week, I met with Megan: a clinical intern who was training to become a counselor. It was a judgment-free zone, and I could tell my therapist Megan about my fears and frustrations, knowing that she'd keep it confidential. More importantly, she helped me learn more about why I ticked in a particular way.

Megan recommended that I read a book called *The Highly Sensitive Person: How to Thrive When the World Overwhelms You* by Elaine Aron, and while I've connected with books before, this book perfectly described how I experienced the world. For highly sensitive people,

- The effects of criticism are especially amplified.
- They're probably used to hearing, "Don't take things so per-

sonally" and "Why are you so sensitive?"
- They feel more deeply.
- They're more emotionally reactive.
- They're empathetic to a fault.

Learning more about this character trait taught me why Sandy Hook had devastated me when others seemed to "move on" from a national tragedy much more quickly. It was such a relief to realize that others operated on this particular wavelength. Working with Megan helped me learn how to navigate through the world and adopt helpful coping strategies. Counseling did not offer a permanent solution to my bouts of anxiousness. Still, it provided me with tools to deal with some of my ongoing struggles.

***

Starting to feel a bit of mental relief, I continued to read as much Marian scholarship as I could get my hands on. Feeling like I was making progress with my research, I asked to meet with Dr. Jansen to talk about some of my ideas. As I talked, I could tell how engaged she was in this particular topic, compared to some of the other ideas I had previously discussed, "There's definitely an idea there – maybe the title will be something like, "The Voice of Mary." She also offered a few suggestions of things to read and left me with these parting words: "Vanessa, you are ready to write your dissertation proposal now. Don't get bogged down by the fear. Just sit down and write it."

At CUA, the dissertation proposal is a two-page plan of a potential dissertation. To anyone who thinks, "How can two pages be that hard? Isn't your dissertation going to be hundreds of pages long?" misses the challenge of the exercise. How does one, at the beginning of an intellectual journey, carefully outline the plan of something that will ultimately take years to write? How can you know where you're going before starting your journey? All of these considerations made the writing process feel overwhelming.

Even before I could write the first draft of the proposal, I had to do a lot of pre-writing. In order to craft a precise sentence that summed up the impetus for a particular chapter, I had to write pages on end. I needed to know that my ideas were feasible, and that I had enough material and research to indicate they would work. This was exponentially harder than comps. It felt like going up a roller coaster. As you get higher and higher, you realize that there's no turning back. *Click-clack, click-clack, click-clack.*

It was my goal of getting the proposal approved by the end of the spring semester. Early twentieth-century Russian novelist Boris Pasternak observed, "No genuine book has a first page. Like the rustling of a forest, it is begotten God knows where, and it grows and it rolls, arousing the dense wilds of the forest until suddenly, in the very darkest, most stunned and panicked moment, it rolls to its end and begins to speak with all the treetops at once." One Saturday morning, I finally took all of the ideas that had been floating in the forest of my head for the past month and let them spill out on the page. Unlike the days where I couldn't hold my focus for more than an hour, on this day, I didn't let myself get up from my chair. I let the ideas pour out all day. Before dinner, I sent Dr. Jansen my first draft, officially kicking off the proposal process.

That first draft was one of six versions that Dr. Jansen read that semester, and while she offered tweaks to tighten my argument, the heart of the document remained faithful to what I had crafted in draft 1. The revision process wasn't as hard as I feared: there needed to be a first draft to get the ball rolling. Once I figured out the structure, everything else started to fall into place.

I had classmates who pushed back on every suggestion from their professors. Ultimately, their unwillingness to change things slowed down their revisions, which stretched out the process for months on end. Moreover, they seemed to be unhappy throughout the entire process. It's not as if I was a doormat, but I learned to choose my battles carefully. If I had a point that I thought was integral to my argument, I fought for it. Writing a dissertation is like playing a game: if you don't follow the rules, you lose. These classmates also embraced negativity and chose to often wallow in their frustration about their progress in the program. While my attitude wasn't completely Pollyanna, I knew that harboring a negative and resentful attitude would hinder my progress and make the entire experience miserable.

***

Therapy was helping me learn to cope with Sandy Hook. Megan had me keep an anxiety journal, in which I identified moments that set off my anxiety. We then reviewed them in therapy and strategize about how to best confront these moments the next time they surfaced. By discussing my concerns aloud, instead of bottling them up inside, I was able to fall asleep at night.

I felt like I was on the upswing when I went to the student union on campus to watch the Boston Marathon on April 15, 2013. Once the elite race was over, I stepped away from the TV and continued to work on my dissertation proposal. I knew I could check online later to see how my friends did, including Jenny, who, in less than two years from becoming a runner, had earned a qualifying time for Boston.

I thought nothing when Jenny called me shortly after she finished her race. "Congratulations!" I said as I picked up the phone.

Instead of cheering, I heard sirens and yelling. "Vanessa, there was a bomb at the end of the race," Jenny said.

What? This didn't make any sense. I asked her to repeat it above the roar of ambulances wailing. "Vanessa, there was some kind of explosion near the finish line. I can't stay on the phone, but I'm okay." She hung up. I ran to the TV in the student lounge, which had a "Breaking News" banner scrolling across - "Bombing at Boston." I stood in my tracks.

As this horrific event played out in real time, the media could only speculate as to what happened. There were pictures of the finish line, a place which had brought such happy memories for me, now engulfed in smoke as paramedics rushed to the aid of the hundreds of spectators who were gravely wounded. The finish line looked more like a warzone than the place that symbolized the triumph of the human spirit.

I took the metro back to Pat's apartment in Vienna and wept the entire ride. This happened to my beloved running community, and I felt helpless.

As the news broke that three people, including eight-year-old Martin Richard, had died, more sobs wracked my body as Pat held me. Emblazoned on the TV was a picture of Martin, a toothy little boy, holding a sign that read, "No more hurting people – peace," which he had made to protest the murder of Trayvon Martin. His innocent plea was unmet, and all of the grief that I had carried for the children of Sandy Hook came flooding back.

The next day, I went to my counselor for my weekly visit. Having talked to Megan about how running was my coping mechanism, she knew that this national disaster, on the heels of the Sandy Hook shooting, was going to be a difficult moment for me.

"Yes, it is absolutely horrific," Megan said, affirming my feelings. "But when you fixate on this and let it consume you, you're not able to function well. That's not meant to diminish your sadness - these are truly horrible events. But being in a place where you're emotionally stuck will not help those who died. You need to start moving forward and learn how to not let these tragedies become all-consuming." She suggested that I cut back on my news intake: "Vanessa, it doesn't mean ignoring the disaster entirely. You need to find some sort of moderation. There becomes a tipping point in which you've learned more than enough to be an informed citizen and then become depressed from such intense media consumption. Each news story is compounding the pain, instead of lessening it." Her words did not mitigate my immediate grief. It took weeks after the bombing to resume a regular sleeping pattern. However, cutting back on my daily news exposure, along with dissecting my feelings with Megan, was helping me learn how to manage my emotions in a conducive manner.

***

In May, the history department's monthly meeting had

scheduled a vote on my dissertation proposal. Seeking a distraction while they met, I grabbed lunch with my friends. Under the auspices of dropping off graded exams to the administrative assistant, I stopped by the department later in the afternoon. When one of my professors informed me that the department approved my proposal, I felt an enormous sense of relief after a year of searching for a specific topic.

A couple of days later, I went out to celebrate with my classmates at San Antonio's, the neighborhood Tex-Mex restaurant. As we enjoyed margaritas and nachos, I got a text from Pat, "Hey – do you want to hang out later tonight?" *Hmm.* He knew I was out with my friends celebrating. I responded, "I'm out now, but should be home around 9. Is that too late?" A few minutes later, he wrote back, "Totally fine! I'll pick you up, and then we can walk around the National Mall, okay?" Sure, it sounded like a nice way to wrap up a celebratory day. By the time I got home, it had started to rain. I half-expected Pat to cancel. But he remained enthusiastic, texting, "It'll be fun!"

All spring, Pat and I talked about our future, including getting engaged. As I put on a nice dress that night, part of me wondered, "Is tonight the night? Is that why Pat didn't cancel?" Perhaps with too much hope, I even took off the Irish Claddagh ring I usually wore on my left ring finger.

As we walked up the marble steps of the Lincoln Memorial, holding umbrellas to shield us from the rain, I felt my heart race – was this really happening? I had always dreamed about getting engaged on the National Mall. I thought it was the most romantic place in D.C. Of course, I never told Pat about this: no one wants a proposal dictated to them. Although we'd visited the Lincoln Memorial together before, this time we carefully read the inscriptions that contained the Gettysburg Address and Lincoln's Second Inaugural Address. Suddenly, Pat raised his voice, "Can I get everyone's attention?" *Oh my gosh, this is really happening.*

In front of a small crowd of curious onlookers, Pat talked about our relationship and our future together. Then, as my heart pounded, he got down on one knee and asked me to marry him. It's the one time in my life where I towered over him (he's nearly a foot taller than me). After I said yes, I also got down on my knees, which put us at the same height. He put his late grandmother's engagement ring on my finger and we kissed and hugged. Everyone clapped and congratulated us. Although it was almost midnight, as we looked over the Reflecting Pool, we called my parents, yelling over the phone, "We're engaged!" But while they were excited, they weren't surprised.

Via Skype, Pat had recently spoken with my parents to ask them for their blessing. Apparently, he asked them a lot of questions, and also expressed to them how committed he was to loving me and taking care of me for the rest of our lives. Pat even asked about how they got engaged. My dad revealed that he proposed to my mom on May 10, 1980. 33 years later to the exact day, on May 10, 2013, Pat proposed to me. From the early months of us dating, Pat told me how much he admired my parents' relationship and viewed that as a model for us to strive for. It was really moving to learn all of this on that special night. After we hung up with my mom and dad, we drove back to Pat's apartment to celebrate, complete with Moët Chandon champagne.

It was a week of two important proposals: one professional, and one incredibly personal. The department said yes to mine, thus setting me on my course to writing a dissertation. And I happily said yes to Pat's, and a few days later, we set a date: May 17, 2014.

Chapter 11: Cumulative Mileage

"In the midst of an ordinary training day, I try to remind
myself that I am preparing for the extraordinary."
– Shalane Flanagan, 2017 New York City Marathon Champion

Pat's Lincoln Memorial proposal left me sky-high, and the
next few days were spent calling family and friends to share
the news. Between the engagement and getting my dissertation
proposal approved, everything felt like it was falling into place.
I naively told my therapist, Megan, that I didn't think we needed
to meet anymore. With misplaced confidence, I thought that I
had finally learned how to manage my anxiety and that true
happiness could override anything.

There were many things related to the wedding that I
looked forward to sharing with my family and dearest friends as
we prepared to get married in my hometown. I had three great
girlfriends who were my bridesmaids, and I asked Kathleen, the
friend I went to for everything, to be my maid of honor. As the
wedding grew closer, I frequently called her, asking questions
ranging from bridesmaids' dresses and makeup to the bigger
questions about getting married and the merging of two families. Kathleen always had an answer or anecdote to everything.

My mom, more adept with Pinterest than I was, eagerly
created various boards to manage centerpieces, flowers, and in-
vitations. I was grateful that she took on the majority of the
wedding planning so that I could focus on my dissertation, as
well as starting my new life with Pat.

***

Shortly after we got engaged, I moved into Pat's apartment. A few months later, we got Heshie, a female English bull-

dog puppy, named after an obscure SNL skit featuring Nasim Pedrad as a middle-aged motivational speaker who gave terrible advice. As a kid, I was not allowed to have a dog, despite my repeated pleas and even circling ads for puppies in the classified ads. Getting Heshie was a childhood dream come true. The day before we picked her up, we went to PetSmart and bought her a leash, pillow, toys, and everything else we thought a dog needed. In an effort to "dog-proof" the apartment, we crawled around on our hands and knees to see what things were easily accessible to a curious and teething pup. As we went to bed that night, I said to Pat, "You know, it'll never just be the two of us again. We'll have Heshie, and then we'll have kids." We knew it was a life-changing moment.

When we picked her up, Heshie was a fluffy chestnut puppy who rode home in the car sitting on my leg, wrapped in a blue blanket. She cried throughout that first night, as it was the first time she was separated from her mother and siblings. We put Heshie's crate next to our bed and Pat slept with one hand in the crate in an attempt to provide some love to our little eight-pound puppy.

All of the rules we initially laid down, such as where she could sit and sleep in the apartment, quickly became relaxed. Heshie's big brown eyes wore us down every time. Through training her, playing with her, taking her for walks, we were slowly becoming a family.

***

Not only was I learning how to take care of a dog, I was also learning how to cook. When I lived with Julie, we made our own separate meals. and because I was cooking only for myself, I tended to rotate a few simple meals that I had no problem eating every three days. Using a small George Foreman grill, I'd cook either pork chops or chicken breasts, usually adding some seasoning, and then either microwave a baked potato or Minute Rice, accompanied by a salad. Although it was incredibly basic, I was fine with this simplicity.

My mom is a fantastic cook, and always makes it look easy.

Although she offered multiple times over the years to show me how, especially as I got older, I always declined. When I moved in with Pat and was responsible for cooking for both of us, I wanted to diversify my meals, and sought her guidance regularly.

After we received some kitchenware from our bridal shower I tried to advance in my culinary abilities. One Saturday night, I wanted to make lasagna. Given that I was more at the spaghetti level, this was a bold move. I had never paid attention when my mom made it, and while the pasta was cooking, I panicked. I didn't even know how to layer the lasagna correctly. Why had I tried to do this without knowing all of the steps? I immediately FaceTimed my mom, so she could see what I was trying (and failing) to do. With eyes like a hawk, she patiently guided me through the remaining steps, likely silently regretting not pushing me more to learn how to cook growing up. The meal was saved, and it would be the first of many times I'd call my mom to come to my culinary rescue.

***

As our wedding approached, and I knew I had to prioritize dissertation work, I didn't feel the urge to set my sights on a goal race for the foreseeable future. Sarah and I amicably ended our coach-athlete partnership. Yet, it was as if the training wheels had come off. I knew what I needed to do to be a good runner, now I needed to figure out what would make me a good writer. And while I stopped doing formal workouts, I ran almost every day, including a 10-mile run on the weekends. It was enough to burn off my nervous energy about the wedding.

I woke up on our wedding day at my childhood house, put on my running clothes, and ran around my neighborhood for four miles, including by the church where we'd pledge to love each other a few hours later. I felt joyful, as if I should've been clanging a bell, yelling, "I'm getting married today!" to anyone I saw. The morning was a flurry of preparations. I anxiously waited to see Pat, but I was hidden away in the back of the church with my bridesmaids and my dad. As the last to depart down the aisle, Kathleen gave me one final hug, and then it was time for my dad and I to enter the church. My dad beamed with pride and joy as he walked me down the aisle. I nearly melted when I saw Pat's face: he radiated pure love. I grinned through the entire ceremony.

A friend of mine from the history department, Fr. Stephen (when you're studying at *The* Catholic University of America, you end up making friends with priests), married us. It was wonderful to have someone we knew officiate our wedding, instead of a stranger. Pat and I held hands and smiled as we listened to Fr. Stephen's homily. As he offered us guidance in our marriage, we occasionally whispered to each other about little things that stood out to us. The one mistake of the day was that in staring into Pat's eyes as we exchanged rings, I accidentally put his gold wedding band on his right hand. He's teased me since that it's the "ring loophole" – an exception that can get him out of any jam in our marriage. We couldn't stop laughing when we realized what happened.

At the reception, Pat's brothers, Jack and Phong gave a lovely joint toast. They, along with their sister, Thao and Pat's parents, made me feel welcome as the newest member of the Corcoran family. After dinner, the rest of the evening was spent on the dance floor. My little cousins, who were five and seven years old, happily danced to every song, and at their request, Pharrell's "Happy" multiple times. I had a sentimental dance with my dad ("Butterfly Kisses" by Bob Carlisle – the song I had known we'd someday dance to since I was 11 years old), while my mom looked on, beaming. Nova and I whooped it up to pop songs we had danced together from CTY years before. Pat and I had a wonderful first dance song – Ray LaMontagne's "You are the Best Thing." When I first heard the song a year before, I loved the lyrics and wanted it to be "our song,"

You are the best thing
(You're the best thing, ooh)
Ever happened to me

Pat said that to me often, and as I danced in his arms, Pat whispered in my ear that our wedding day was "our best day yet." I couldn't have agreed more.

***

Pat was so supportive of the teaching and leadership opportunities that came my way that he was willing to postpone our honeymoon for three months while I did one last summer at CTY. At last, we set sail to the Bahamas on our honeymoon cruise. The trip was incredibly refreshing, especially after an intense summer of work.

It was the first vacation we had ever taken together, and as we pulled away from the boardwalk, we breathed in the sea air and felt all of our worries evaporate. It was peaceful to sit out on our balcony and watch the land slowly vanish over the horizon, holding hands as we reclined in our deck chairs, completely disconnected from the world. We took a selfie on our first night on the ship, grinning widely for the camera, as the setting sun made our faces glow even brighter. It was with that joy that we returned to Washington a week later: tan, well-rested, and excited about starting our new lives together.

***

Since I submitted my proposal in May 2013, it had been over a year since I had a tangible deadline. Seeking some public accountability during the Fall 2014 semester, I agreed to participate in my department's colloquium series. Participants were required to write a full-length chapter (about 50 pages) to be read in advance by fellow graduate students and professors. Subsequently, I'd participate in a two-hour workshop, where people brought questions and suggestions that emerged from their careful readings of my chapter. I knew that this would be a nerve-wracking exercise but hoped that the benefits would outweigh these drawbacks.

In *Bird by Bird: Some Instructions on Writing and Life*, Anne Lamott wrote, "Almost all good writing begins with terrible first efforts. You need to start somewhere." For two months, I vigorously wrote and edited my first chapter, which examined how medieval devotional materials described the marriage of Joseph and the Virgin Mary, as well as liturgical dramas that were performed in large cities in the later Middle Ages (approximately 1200-1500 C.E.). I observed that these sources imagined Mary and Joseph in heated verbal conflict following Mary revealing to him that she was pregnant. One English play featured Joseph in a 75-line monologue lamenting that he had married a "wench for a wife." I was stunned to see such charged language when describing the Holy Family. I compared these sources with medieval advice manuals designed to counsel wives on their behavior. Wives were to show deference to their husbands in all aspects of their marriages. For example, a fourteenth-century text called *The Good Wife's Guide* advised women, "Do not be arrogant or answer back to your future husband or to his words and do not contradict him, especially in front of others." It was fascinating material, and I enjoyed discovering new sources to include in the chapter.

After a few months of writing and revising, I sent it off the draft to the department. I felt naked and vulnerable knowing that so many people were going to read my work. At these workshops, I'd seen classmates who were either ill-prepared or thrown off guard by the barrage of feedback and criticism. I didn't want the same thing to happen to me, and my stomach twisted into a knot of nerves whenever I thought about my upcoming presentation.

During the colloquium, both my classmates and professors seemed interested in the material, especially the colorful language and unique portrayals of the Virgin Mary. However, I faced lots of questions and suggestions about the structure of the chapter. The common consensus among the professors was that I consider restructuring the entire framework of my dissertation to make for a stronger argument. I was completely taken aback. *Restructure the whole thing?* I already had a rough outline of the overall trajectory of the dissertation. *It's going to take months, maybe even a year, to do that – how will I ever finish?* As I tried to process the discussion, I worried that the senior thesis episode would return to haunt me, that just like at Holy Cross, I'd work to craft a project that would ultimately be deemed "unsatisfactory."

I felt overwhelmed as I walked home from the metro. My steps grew slower as I felt weighed down by the work I knew I had to do to reshape the dissertation. I was exhausted from the day. Moreover, I was exhausted from thinking about what work still needed to be done. I had never worked so long or so hard for something: yet it remained unclear whether I'd ever finish it. The song "They Just Keep Moving the Line" from the TV show "Smash," ran through my head. The lyrics perfectly described my never-ending quest to receive approval from my professors,

So I made friends with rejection
I've straightened up my spine!
I'll change each imperfection
Till it's time to drink the wine!
I'd toast to resurrection
But they just keep moving the line!
Please give me some direction,
'Cause they just keep moving the line!

The following day, I went to Dr. Davis's office to follow up on a few lingering questions: I was worried that this was a big setback. I started to ramble: babbling a mile a minute. Finally, Dr. Davis politely interrupted me, "Vanessa, I hope you know that this was a good outcome. You want people to give you feedback, and you really have something here. It's a first draft – we don't expect perfection. The important thing is that you keep going." Her perspective offered the clarity I needed. But, it took a few weeks to feel ready to tackle it again. Instead, I focused on helping my Junior Seminar students successfully reach the end of the semester. Plus, with Christmas coming up, I happily welcomed the distraction the holiday season brought as an excuse to put the dissertation on hold.

***

Christmas is my favorite time of the year, and my love for it stemmed from our family traditions. Nova and I decorated a gingerbread house, each responsible for half of the house, often resulting in eclectic-looking houses. Every year, we watched "A

Muppet Christmas Carol," my dad's all-time favorite movie. My mom baked half a dozen kinds of cookies, which we either enjoyed as dessert, or when we grew older, as breakfast on Christmas Day. The Saturday after Thanksgiving was always spent decorating our tree, listening to Christmas carols as we worked. Our family Christmas tree is a wonderful mixture of ornaments that Nova and I made when we were little, as well as souvenirs that we brought home from family vacations, a tradition Nova and I continued as we began to travel on our own.

It was our first married Christmas together, and I happily threw myself into preparing for the holidays. Mining my mom's favorite recipes and calling her for advice, I baked dozens of cookies, carefully learning the insider tricks to baking gluten-free with only a few gingerbread men fatalities. I decorated our tree and apartment with as much décor as I could find at Target under $100, knowing that we primarily relied on Pat's salary and I shouldn't be too frivolous. Each morning, I turned on the Christmas tree and put on holiday music to play all day long, creating a miniature Winter Wonderland that mirrored the magic of my childhood home.

Even though it was the first time I was away from my family for the holidays, Pat and I had such a wonderful time celebrating that it made the distance seem bearable. In our holiday best, we went to Christmas Mass, listening to the brass quintet and the choir that played all the traditional Christmas hymns, including my personal favorite, "O Come All Ye Faithful." After we opened our presents from each other, we FaceTimed with my parents. As we drank coffee and ate Christmas cookies, Pat and I were both grinning from ear to ear. The feelings of peace and joy that we shared were better than any present wrapped under the tree.

***

A few days after the holidays, I flew to Dayton, Ohio for a two-week research trip at the International Marian Research Institution at the University of Dayton. This research center housed the largest collection of archival materials on the Virgin

Mary, including some sixteenth-century prayer guides I hoped would factor into my dissertation. I wished that the center was located in Italy, as the entire trip was paid for by a research grant that I had won. Instead of knowing that my *per diem* went toward local Italian pizza, wine, and gelato, I instead resigned myself to the fact that the closest I'd come to Italian cuisine was the nearby Olive Garden. Nevertheless, I excitedly viewed the research stint as a writer's retreat.

After I picked up my rental car and drove to the Marriott Residence, my home for the next two weeks, I optimistically wrote about my goals for the trip:

I am trying to envision the finish line, even though it is over a year away. I'm going to be counting on more people for help, support, and encouragement, than I've ever asked for. Otherwise, if I let it all fester in my head, I'll burn out way too soon.

I want to finish. I need to keep reminding myself that I want this to happen.

For the next two weeks, I'll either be in the library or in my hotel room, with my laptop as my one companion. I need to be productive and crank out some decent material.

I hope I can one day fondly look back at this trip. I hope I'll be able to remember sessions of solid writing and innovative thinking. When future grad students ask for advice, I want to cite this trip as inspiration, recalling with a smile, "I wrote a new draft of my chapter, and it changed my mentality for the dissertation in the final stretch."

***

That optimism and determination carried me throughout the trip. On the seventh floor of the Roesch Library, I had a table all to myself at the Marian Library. Although occasionally a librarian would check in with me to see if I needed anything, I otherwise worked completely undisturbed. Any book I needed on the history of Marian devotion was within a 20-foot radius, and I finally had the headspace to grapple with the prospect of revising the structure of my dissertation.

When the archives closed at 5 p.m., I went for a run

around campus, and then drove back to the hotel to clean up. For dinner, I rotated through a set of chain restaurants that were within walking distance of the Marriott. I'd spend a couple of hours writing while I ate, expanding on my thoughts that emerged during the day's reading. The waiter gave me endless refills of Diet Coke, caffeinating my brain after a long day of critical thinking and writing. I had nothing else to do but dissertation work: no laundry, no chores, no cooking. Taking away all of those responsibilities and expectations enabled me to clear my head and focus solely on my research.

***

At the end of my trip, I packed up everything that had been strewn about in my hotel room, returned the car, and waited for my flight to take off. As I sat in the terminal, a four-hour delay gave me time to think about how to plan for the next few months.

It was time to bring in the big guns: my mom and aunts. My aunts, Barbara and Maryanne, have been involved in my life since I was born. Whenever they called to check up on me during my college years, they gave boyfriend advice, career suggestions, and occasionally an unsolicited $20, "so you can do something fun with your friends." Before I boarded my flight, I emailed them,

I've always tried to hold myself accountable and to uphold certain standards. However, I've come to realize that I need a little more help to make sure I do this consistently. I need to be more specific than "I am going to work on my dissertation today." While I accomplish things each day, I need more of a strategic approach to getting this thing done. It is a new year - why not use this time to really resolve to change my writing habits? You all are such go-getters - some regular accountability will do me some good!

It was my hope to ride the momentum wave I had created during my research trip. I asked them to help keep me accountable about both my daily and long-term writing goals, as well as the regular obstacles I faced. I created a writing contract that I hoped would ensure that it would be a productive semester:

- *During the week, I will commit to at least 3 thirty-minute writing sessions.*
- *On the weekend, I will commit to at least one hour-long writing session.*
- *At the beginning of the week, I will plan out concrete goals and email them out to you.*
- *I will update my bibliography on a semi-weekly basis.*

It was with that support network, as well as the encouragement from Dr. Jansen that I needed to "break the back of Chapter 1," that I set to work, optimistic about the road ahead.

Chapter 12: Dream Deferred

"Sometimes the moments that challenge us the most define us." – Deena Kastor, 2004 Olympic Marathon Bronze Medalist

I took my writing contract and used it to guide my daily routine. Each morning, I emailed my mom and aunts, detailing my goals for the day, such as what I aimed for on January 27, 2015:

- *read* Speaking in the Medieval World *by Jean E. Godsall-Myers*
- *outline and write 3 pages for historiography section of introduction*
- *start outlining speech section for Chapter 1 (and try to write two pages if there's time)*

I primarily worked from home, and I was grateful that Pat was able to financially support me while I focused on my dissertation. After Pat left for work; I fed and walked Heshie, and then settled down with my laptop for a few hours. When I felt that my energy was flagging, I either did household chores or went out for a run. Then back to writing, make dinner, and try to wrap things up for the day before Pat came home. It often felt like the movie *Groundhog's Day*, with little variation in the routine. Although I was slowly starting to get some writing done, the monotony also wore me down. The winter sky was grey, and more often than not, matched my mood and feelings towards this seemingly-stagnant process. I was starting to slowly descend into a downward spiral of anxiety and self-doubt. Each episode of panic started to build upon the next, making me unable to be productive or feel optimistic that I'd ever finish.

***

To unwind at night, I was re-reading Kathrine Switzer's *Marathon Woman*. As I read about her preparation for the 1974 Boston marathon, one particular passage stood out to me,

"One snowy Sunday in February I jogged up to Central Park to do my long run...I was the only person in the park...I looked up at the expensive apartments along Fifth Avenue, imagining the people having coffee or Bloody Marys', reading their thick Sunday editions of the New York Times, or looking out the window and watching this solitary figure running through the snow...The fact was I wanted just for once to curl up on a Sunday with coffee and *The New York Times*. That's when I knew I was tired. So I stopped for a moment and shouted up to the buildings, 'There will be a time in my life when I don't have to prove myself anymore!'"

I instantly related to this sentiment. It was the late nights and early mornings staring at the blinking cursor on my laptop, trying to knock out a few more pages that made me wonder if taking on this marathon of a project was worth it. I also grew frustrated having to answer, with a forced smile at parties and department functions, "So, when do you think you'll be done?"

I inwardly sighed as I launched into my canned response. It was my hope to defend in 2016, which meant I'd earn my Ph.D. before turning 30. But there were many days when I wanted to curl up with coffee and a fun book without my inner voice nagging, "You could be writing now..."

I hoped that when I finally defended my dissertation, that the desperate feeling of seeking approval would at last disappear. Until then, like Kathrine Switzer, I wanted to shout to the rooftops, "There will be a time in my life when I don't have to prove myself anymore!"

***

That February, I read an article by Marian scholar Dr. Kati Inhat entitled "Marian Liturgies and Marian Miracles in the Benedictine Tradition of post-Conquest England." As I read her analysis of one of the sources that was integral to my dissertation, some of the comments that Dr. Inhat made started to sound too familiar. Did she already make part of my argument?

My nervous reaction to the book was justified. One of the most fascinating stories Dr. Jansen told us in one of our seminars had to do with the idea of multiple discovery: different scholars writing about similar ideas in parallel. In 1986, women's historian Caroline Walker Bynum was working on her latest book: *Holy Feast and Holy Fast: The Religious Significance of Food to Medieval Women*. Through reading sources about religious women who participated in extreme fasting as an act of pious devotion, Bynum argued "medieval people often saw gluttony as the major form of lust, fasting as the most painful renunciation, and eating as the most basic and literal way of encountering God." Close to the book's publication, Bynum received word that a similar book was also about to be published.

Bynum learned that an Italian historian named Rudolph Bell was writing a book entitled *Holy Anorexia*. His study investigated these same fasting practices from a psychological perspective. Using the modern clinical definition of anorexia, Bell examined 170 holy women, more than half of whom; he concluded, "displayed clear signs of anorexia." Ultimately, both books made significant and unique contributions to the study of women's religious experiences in the Middle Ages. One piece of scholarship did not cancel the other out. Yet, one can imagine the authors' dread as they learned of this news.

I kept reading, closely, waiting to see where Dr. Ihnat's argument went. Whoosh! She made a slight intellectual turn and focused on a different subset of Marian devotion than my own research. Once the knot in my stomach unraveled, I went back and started reading the article from the beginning. Still, each academically-induced day of panic stretched on relentlessly.

***

Working on my dissertation drained me of all my energy. This wasn't the blissful exhaustion that came from a 2-mile run. I was worn out.

While my parents and Pat knew that I was struggling to make progress in my dissertation writing, I did not reveal the extent to which this stagnation had depressed me. I hid it all. I didn't tell anyone about the time, when, after staring blankly at my laptop for 30 minutes, I typed "THIS ISN'T WORKING. WHAT'S WRONG WITH ME?" silently yelling at myself for another failed writing session.

Because Pat was supporting us, and I had a small tuition stipend, I didn't have to work that semester. "You're incredibly lucky," my professors said, "You can write all day long. What an opportunity." I understood that it was a privilege, but I missed teaching and my students. I also appreciated that teaching used to break up the monotony of the day. Now, when the to-do list was "just write," I felt isolated and unproductive.

With no reason to go to campus, I usually stayed at home. I didn't get dressed - why would I need to if I wasn't seeing anyone? Instead, I wore sweatpants and hooded sweatshirts, often pulling the large hood around my head while I wrote, as if to envelop myself in a cocoon. I couldn't wait each day until Pat came home – his eternal optimism and willingness to support me buoyed me that winter. He made it clear that he wanted me to be happy, regardless if I finished or not.

I was in a dark place, and as much as I attempted to patch up the holes of its previous iteration, a black cloud enlarged each time. What I had done was dangerous. I had placed all of my hope for happiness and satisfaction in finishing. "I'll be happy once I have my Ph.D.," I'd say to myself, but was uncertain if that was ever possible.

I was lying to everyone. I'd find one anecdote of positivity or productivity, and give it as much leverage as possible whenever I saw my professors. There were even times when Dr. Jansen said, "I know you're always going to be responsible and stay on top of things." The picture I was painting for her did not match my reality.

I felt like such a failure in school, and that feeling colored my entire identity. I had no other academic training or professional experience. Quitting the program didn't feel like an option either.

I both wanted to die and was horrified that the idea had entered into my mind. I knew I couldn't go through with it - I knew that it would devastate Pat and my family. Years before, when I was going off to college, my mom, recalling a friend who lost a brother to suicide, told me: "No grade is that important. You could not ever disappoint us." And to underscore her point, she added, "if you ever thought about that, know that I couldn't imagine being on this earth without you."

A decade later, the comment stuck with me and caused me to never put a plan into action. Despite her plea, I secretly hoped some sort of terrible accident would happen. Maybe I'd get hit by a car or get cancer - that way, it wouldn't be my fault. I'd be finally released from this misery. These intrusive thoughts played in my head on a loop. I had had these thoughts before in fleeting moments of depression, but had never faced them so regularly as I had that winter.

Rationally, I knew that these depressing thoughts were cries for help. Yet, I'd repeatedly tell myself, "Your problems aren't that bad. People are dealing with real issues: money, family, sickness - this is just school. You need to get over it." Had a loved one told me they felt like this, I would've taken those cries for help seriously. But I bottled it up and tried to put on a brave face.

I continued to be a good actor. At school functions, I'd smile and engage with my classmates and professors, providing assurances that I was writing. To them, I had just gotten married, was teaching, running, doing all of the right things. They had no reason to suspect I was unhappy beyond the usual grad school angst.

One devastating news story in the running community snapped me back to reality. Madison Holleran, a first-year student and track athlete at UPenn, jumped off of a nine-story parking garage. When her family found her journal, it said, "No, no more help." Madison grew up with a loving family and large circle of friends, all of whom struggled to cope with her shocking passing. In the weeks that followed, they tried to piece together what pushed Madison to make this ultimate, irrevocable decision. I cried while I read about her, especially because so much of Madison's life mirrored my own. I knew what it felt like to have a black spot that clouded my ability to feel joy.

Although I knew my actions differed from Madison's, it pained me that I kept opening my thoughts up to such dark thoughts. "This is not normal," I'd think to myself. Even so, I remained enshrouded in darkness, and ashamed to tell anyone.

***

After months of slogging away, I turned in my first chapter at the end of May, but worried that it wouldn't be deemed good enough. A few weeks later, an email arrived from Dr. Jansen: "Vanessa, I am encouraged by what I have read thus far. I think you are off to a good start." Moreover, she thought that subsequent chapters would be easier to write now that I figured out my writing routine. I couldn't stop smiling. It was the happiest I had felt in months. I attributed my depression to the wintry weather and struggles with my dissertation. Now that it was summer and I seemed to be on the upswing, I once again foolishly thought I had put the worst of it behind me.

While I was drafting Chapter 2, my old roommate Julie was making enormous strides in her dissertation, preparing to defend in Fall 2015. We spent much of the summer writing together. I lived for our writing dates, for both the progress we made in our writing, and for the company. When we shared an apartment, Julie and I had written together often enough that we knew how to balance intense periods of silent writing punctuated by quick breaks of rapid-fire conversation. Julie was my dissertation role model: no one had moved through our program as quickly as she did. Moreover, she managed to write efficiently *and* have a social life.

Each week, Julie and I picked a different coffee shop, rotating through our favorite locations throughout Washington. After ordering large coffees, we'd grab a table big enough for our laptops, notebooks, and any relevant reading materials. Sitting across from each other, we'd open our matching white Mac-

Books, as if we were about to square off in a game of Battleship, and begin typing away. After 90 minutes of writing, we shut our computers for ten minutes, and chatted about our writing or our plans for the weekend. When it was time to get back to work, we were vigilant about staying focused. Neither of us wanted to be the one to break up the flow of productivity. Julie's presence incentivized me to not check my email or Facebook. Her presence also made the writing process, which was usually a solitary endeavor, feel a little less lonely. Julie knew how to offer positivity, and could challenge me to work harder.

Our writing meetings often happened on Saturday mornings: a time when much of Washington opted for long brunches, replete with bottomless Mimosas or Bloody Marys. I sometimes looked at them jealously: they looked as if they didn't have a care in the world. I had made the choice to pursue my doctorate. Even so, when I saw people out having fun, I couldn't help but yearn for a time when the dissertation was no longer one of the main aspects of my life.

***

Even though I was trying to focus on my work and making concrete steps towards finishing my chapters, I continued to face bouts of sleeplessness. It was bad enough to be plagued with thoughts of self-doubt and failure during the day, but then to have them playing out on a repeat track in the wee hours of the morning was torture:

Are you ever going to finish?
What will you do if you drop out?
Are you going to be able to get a job?
You're not getting anything done that's worth showing to your professors.
What if the department recommends you leave the program?
You're going to fail.
The department is going to find some way to quietly encourage you to leave.
You'll need to explain to everyone that the Ph.D. didn't work out.

Again and again and again. After a sleepless night, I'd wake up feeling sluggish and unable to immediately dive into work. As a morning person, this was especially damning, and those foggy mornings felt like a second dose of punishment.

I could even validate my doubts in statistics. Only 57% of people who start a Ph.D. program finish within ten years. I also personally knew people who didn't finish, who either chose to walk away or were strongly encouraged to take the exit package of a master's degree and cut their losses. They went on to do other things, but I really didn't want that for myself. But I feared that washing out could become a real possibility.

My mind was my worst enemy. Eleanor Roosevelt said, "No one can make you feel inferior without your consent." I often felt like a failure, more often than anyone else thought I was performing poorly. I thought I could conquer my anxiety by simply performing better, thus banishing the negative demons away.

As I prepared for meetings with my professors, my heart raced and my mouth grew dry. Sometimes I felt nauseous, other times my breathing grew shallow. Even if the meeting went well, the build-up to the day was miserable. The negative chatter in my head was getting in the way of my happiness.

***

I submitted my second chapter in early September. While I waited for Dr. Jansen's feedback, I moved onto tackling my next chapter, hoping that I could create some semblance of momentum. As Pat and I were getting ready to start a movie, I saw an email from Dr. Jansen pop up as we were about to start a movie.

"Vanessa, I think the chapter landed in my inbox a bit too prematurely," she wrote.

I burst into tears. It was like a damn had broken wide-open. Any repaired confidence I had shattered. This feedback was proof that I could not write a passable dissertation. More than any other moment, this dark phase threatened to end the goal I had worked toward my entire adult life. This moment represented an amalgamation of all of my past failures: the senior thesis from Holy Cross, my struggles with Latin, and my continued attempts to make my writing meet the standards set forth by my professors. Once again, my anxiety and insecurities stood as barriers that prevented me from advancing in my professional career.

I blamed myself for not seeking another career path. Surely, I could've found gainful employment in a different field. However, since my first semester of college, I had set my sights on earning my Ph.D. I didn't see another option on the table. What was I going to do? What was my identity without academia? I feared this was a tipping point and a clear indication that I could wash out of graduate school without finishing the dissertation.

I called my parents in tears, "What if I don't finish? Will you still support me if I drop out?" Without a moment of hesitation, they replied, "You know we love you no matter what. But we also know that you can finish. You've always managed to pull yourself out of these tough spots, and we know you'll do it again." I needed them to promise that I'd have their support regardless if I finished or walked away.

Getting into fix-it mode, Pat immediately wanted to figure out a solution. He had seen me confront anxiety for years and knew that this was a breaking point. As I wept, Pat searched online for a psychiatrist, and made an appointment with a Dr. Turner whose office was within walking distance of our new apartment in Dupont Circle.

Two days later, I sat in her waiting room, shifting nervously in my seat. Dr. Turner brought an air of calm as soon as she entered the room. Her voice was soothing as she asked, "What brings you here today, Vanessa?"

I had lived an anxious life yet was unwilling to connect the dots. I had chalked up each stressful episode to be an isolated incident. Bu in reality, each incident was part of a larger pattern.

My anxiety, it turns out, was not a product of graduate school. It was a shadow that had followed me since I was a child. I wasn't just someone who "got stressed." My anxiety and difficulty sleeping were real issues that required external help. Equally as concerning, they threatened to demolish everything I had worked for. I needed to acknowledge that my anxiety had a genuine and adverse impact on my life. I also needed to recognize that anxiety was not something to be ashamed about. I had to learn how to manage it in order to have my head clear enough to tackle the dissertation. I wanted to live my life without this dark cloud following me.

I had seen a counselor several years before, which was helpful in the short-term. However, there was clearly a long-term problem that I couldn't fix by myself. While it was easy to point to the dissertation as the immediate root of my anxiety and sleep issues, these problems had followed me for years. As I spoke to Dr. Turner, all of these stories spilled out. I told her of all the times growing up and in college, that my head games and recurring thoughts of doubt, threatened to spin out of my control, only to reach a devastating magnitude in grad school. She ultimately concluded that I needed to go on two types of medication to help combat my now officially-diagnosed clinical anxiety.

The diagnosis was both painful and liberating (although it would be a long time before I saw it in that way). These intrusive thoughts went imposter syndrome: these were real issues that had radically shaped my life. "You need to take this diagnosis seriously," said Dr. Turner "We can find a way out of this together, but it's going to take time and hard work." I had to regularly journal about my daily anxieties: what triggered them, how I responded, and then ways to differently handle those moments of panic the next time they resurfaced. Although it was hard to read all these in quick succession, reviewing them with a careful eye helped me to identify some of the regular patterns around these moments.

Dr. Turner warned me that there would be an adjustment period before the medication began to kick in. The first two weeks days were rough. I lost my appetite and stumbled through the days feeling sluggish. Trazodone helped me fall and stay asleep, but I'd wake up the next morning feeling hungover for a couple of hours. I was in a stupor: drained from the emotional rollercoaster that I had been on with my dissertation.

***

Two weeks later, my old roommate Julie defended her dissertation and graduated with distinction. The entire history department heaped enormous praises upon her and Julie had earned every accolade bestowed on her. I knew first-hand how hard she worked and was incredibly proud of her. I still looked at my own efforts as second-rate and that I'd never achieve success comparable to that of Julie. I had it in my head that my professors regarded my classmates: Julie, and Sarah, who had defended the year before, as the ones with the most promise. I, on the other hand, felt like a second-rate student. Professors liked me enough, but it never felt like they viewed me as promising as my classmates.

A few weeks after her defense, Julie pulled me aside. "You'll make it here too, Vanessa," she said. Julie knew me so well that she could tell I was struggling to stay afloat. "Keep your head down and keep going."

A month later, I started sleeping through the night more consistently. The sleeping medication started to take the edge off so I could sleep. I also benefited from visiting Dr. Turner for regular counseling sessions. Talking through my fears, instead of keeping them bottled up, lifted a weight off my shoulders. Finding a way to manage my sleep made it possible to tackle the other concerns in turn.

As I sought to put back the pieces and salvage the remainder of the semester, I opted to throw myself into preparing for the class I'd be teaching in the following semester: The History of the Crusades. Rationally, I knew that Dr. Jansen wouldn't have recommended me to teach at the University of Maryland if she didn't have confidence in me. Rather than sitting at home, feeling useless and unproductive, I could put together lectures on the rise of Islam, the 1st Crusade, and the importance of Jerusalem to Christianity, Judaism, and Islam. It was a welcome distraction. Moreover, it followed some of the advice Dr. Jansen gave, "Put at a couple of weeks between you and the latest draft. Then go back. Read it out loud. It will be easier to see where you need to revise."

***

I couldn't deny any longer that my writing needed improvement. Following a suggestion from Julie, I made an appointment to see Dr. Kevin Rulo, the director of our university's Writing Center. In our first meeting, I brought Dr. Jansen's feedback on Chapter 2. Patiently, Dr. Rulo had me work through her feedback line by line, and pointed out that in my state of despair, I had missed lines such as, "You've got some good material that is waiting to be molded into a coherent structure, held together by a strong argument." In solely focusing on the criticism, I couldn't see that Dr. Jansen had also offered words of encouragement.

Although he didn't know my topic that well, Dr. Rulo helped me work on tweaking thesis statements and brainstorming new ways to conceptualize the organization of the chapter. For an hour once a week, we'd discuss three pages. In the grand scheme of the dissertation, that may seem small, but we got a lot of mileage out of those three pages. More than that, we'd explore ideas for additional segments of each chapter and work carefully to tighten up my argument. These fascinating conversations helped me to finally make some concrete progress.

A year before, I would've been embarrassed to admit that I was going to the Writing Center. *Shouldn't I, as a doctoral candidate, be prepared to write solo?* No! Professors ask their colleagues to look over their manuscripts all the time. Writing should never be a solo endeavor. To expect good writing to emerge when written in a vacuum is futile. Asking for feedback is a natural part of the process. I was finally learning that there is no shame in asking for any kind of support.

Although combing through my college journal in therapy highlighted moments of extreme worry, it also captured a moment of positivity that motivated me to keep going. Three months into my time at Holy Cross, I wrote, "I think I'm going to get my doctorate in history." I owed it to that optimistic eighteen-year-old to see this dream to its fruition.

I started running more regularly, having let it fall by the wayside for the past year. I thought that backing away from running was the responsible thing to do when I needed to focus on my dissertation. I didn't realize that running was part of the glue that was holding my sanity intact.

Once the medication started to help me sleep more consistently, I resumed running regularly. In doing so, I started to feel like my old self again. Having recently moved to Dupont Circle, we now lived near the Capital Crescent Trail: a ten-mile paved path that stretched from Georgetown to Bethesda. After running through the city, weaving around pedestrians and ducking cars that failed to use the turn signal, my shoulders relaxed as I entered the peaceful trail. This shared-use path offered long stretches of shade and respite from cars and the noise pollution of downtown Washington. I was coming up for air after being underwater for months.

***

When you've been told that your work isn't "quite there yet," it's hard to regain confidence to believe in yourself again. It took months of going back to the drawing board, trying to better articulate my argument in this chapter and show its merit to my project at large.

I was nearly at the point where I could feel ready to submit it again. After spending a semester revising Chapter 2, I did my final read-through at Julie's apartment at the end of May. "Vanessa, you're stalling. You need to turn it in and get this off your plate," Julie encouraged me, giving me some tough love. I needed to overcome my fear of rejection and submit my chapter. I said a silent prayer as I clicked "send."

I turned 30 on June 19, 2016. My parents came into town for the weekend, and we had a party on the rooftop of our apartment building with my friends from grad school. My parents gave me a bracelet with the inscription, "It's a marathon, not a sprint." It couldn't have been a more appropriate gift. I knew I would wear it for inspiration during my daily writing sessions. We watched the sunset over Rock Creek Park: I loved ringing in a new decade with some of my dearest loved ones. My only ambivalence toward this particular birthday was that for years, I had it in my head that I would finish my dissertation *before* turning 30. My parents reminded me, I'd likely finish and walk before my next birthday. It didn't matter *when* I finished: it solely mattered *that* I finished.

After a few hours of cleaning up from the birthday weekend, I opened my email to find a response from Dr. Jansen, "Vanessa, it's a big improvement over the earlier draft I read…Now all it needs is a bit of prose polishing."

Dr. Jansen's response was the best birthday present I could've asked for. It didn't completely eliminate the darkness, but I started to see a glimmer of hope and a light at the end of the long tunnel.

Chapter 13: Operation Endgame

"Never give up on your dreams, but also never give up working to make your dream become a reality." – Meb Keflezighi, 2004 Olympic Silver Medalist, Winner of the 2014 Boston Marathon

In the summer of 2016, I was laser focused on finishing my dissertation. I was starting to learn how to manage my anxiety and regain the confidence that I needed to finish this endurance challenge. My only job was to write. Although that solitary task of writing was daunting a year before, I finally had honed in on my argument. I claimed that by analyzing late medieval characterizations of Mary's voice as powerful and authoritative, it reflected widespread concerns for regulating women's speech in the Middle Ages and served as an effective barometer for measuring both religious and social change.

I was fascinated to examine the power of one woman's voice, especially in a world that viewed women's speech with a fair amount of skepticism. The irony wasn't lost on me that I was writing in an age where women are repeatedly shushed or cut off when speaking, or when they dare to speak out, they're decried as "bossy," "shrill," and "ambitious." Although my research on the suppression of women's voices was confined to the Middle Ages, watching Donald Trump leer and stomp around the debate stage while Hillary Clinton spoke, I felt that the topic of silencing women had particular resonance in the present day.

At last, I started to have clear goals for the months that lay ahead of me. I finally knew how to manage long writing sessions. Running helped to break up the monotony. As the summer progressed, I kept writing and running: each goal sharpened my focus for the other.

In an effort to get back into shape, I signed up for the Navy-Air Force Half Marathon in September. Although I hadn't been training as seriously as I was a few years before, I wanted to sign up for a longer race to see how close I could get to my PR (1:32:33). I spent a lot of that summer exploring the trails of Rock Creek Park, which was just minutes away from our apartment. I love Rock Creek Park because it is an oasis in the middle D.C. It had been sweltering all summer in Washington, and Rock Creek Park offered much-needed refuge. Especially at dusk, the trees created extra shade and helped drop the temperature.

One night, after I had written a few pages examining the complexities of the Virgin Mary operating as both Queen of Heaven and Empress of Hell (both titles ascribed to her in medieval devotional narratives), I needed to put away the laptop for an hour. The temperature was mercifully cooler, and for the first time in weeks, my face wasn't beet-red after a mere fifteen minutes of running. It felt idyllic and the run ultimately worked its magic. The swarm of thoughts I had about organizing this subsection of my chapter quieted down.

***

I wrote a lot that summer. The writing wasn't always eloquent, but I wrote nearly every day. I had wished it came as naturally to me as running did. Still, I finally felt like I was in the writing groove. The mile markers indicated that I was getting closer to the finish line.

In the middle of August, I submitted my third chapter, which was both the most enjoyable and quickest to write. It was an examination of the seemingly-opposed titles of Mary as Queen of Heaven and Empress of Hell. The woman traditionally viewed as the serene Madonna was viewed in medieval sources as powerful enough to help the faithful evade damnation in hell and ascend to heaven. I found fascinating illuminated manuscripts that depicted Mary wrestling demons and chastising the devil as "a wicked thief." Finally, I was mentally unblocked, and the writing flowed out onto the page. I finally figured out how to structure my argument and write efficiently. By aiming for quality over quantity, my writing improved.

***

The day before the Navy-Air Force Half Marathon, amid a three-mile easy run, I did a couple of sprints at race pace (7:00/mile), which felt fast. I wondered whether my goal was overly ambitious. Sometimes you have to take the risk and go for broke, and that's what I settled on as I created my pace band with projected mile splits.

As the starting gun went off, the song they played at the start was "September" by Earth, Wind, and Fire: the song we walked into at our wedding reception. Thinking of Pat made me smile as I crossed the starting line. Knowing that 7:02-7:03 pace would net me a PR, I ran around seven-minute miles consistently for the first part of the race. As I ran, I wondered, "Is this a reasonable pace or will I eventually run out of steam?" I hoped for the former and pressed on.

Although the pack of runners spread out within a couple of miles, there were still enough people around to work on picking off other runners throughout the course. Those early miles clicked off easily. By mile 7, however, it started to take a lot more effort to hit this pace, and the exertion had taken its toll. I was wondering if I should try to slow down, but feared that if I did, I wouldn't be able to get back my momentum. I opted to press on, crossing my fingers that the fast pace was sustainable. The volunteers at the water stations were amazing. As they whooped and hollered at mile 8, they offered a shot of adrenaline when I really needed it.

At mile 9, a man sidled up next to me, "You ladies are fast! I don't know how you do it." I didn't have the energy to explain that yes, many women can run as fast, if not faster, than men. I opted instead to simply smile, slowly pulling away, until I passed him for good at mile 10.

Knowing that Pat was waiting for me at mile 11 gave me a push to slog through the final 5k. I was getting so tired. Pat cheered and yelled as I ran by: I could only muster a brief wave to him. The finish line in front of the Washington Monument, loomed ahead out of reach. As I could finally see the clock appear, I knew a PR wasn't a far-off dream, but a reality. I proudly pumped my fist with a huge smile on my face as I crossed the finish line.

Finishing time: 1:32:17 (7:02 pace)
Overall place: 126/5,220 (overall)

It was one of the most evenly paced races I had ever run. Pat was impressed that I came within 10 seconds of my predicted finishing time. I told him at that point, with nearly one hundred races under my belt, it became a lot easier to be consistent.

It was my first PR in almost three years. All of those hours of running had shifted into writing time, which made complete sense, given that the more important goal was completing the Ph.D. For the past couple of years, when people had asked about my running, I always couched it with, "Yes, I'm running a lot, but not training for anything. I'm trying to focus on finishing my dissertation." What I should have said was, "I'm running consistently and do have some long-term goals. While my running schedule isn't as regimented as it used to be, I've learned how to manage my training and make my running time as effective as it can be." This flexible approach led me to a new half-marathon PR and gave me the confidence that my fastest years weren't behind me.

**

At the beginning of the Fall 2016 semester, Dr. Jansen said that we ought to meet in the coming weeks to discuss my "endgame" – the final stages of my dissertation. Although I had been telling people that I planned to graduate in the spring of 2017, I always said this with some trepidation. Whenever imposter syndrome took over, I even feared that while my committee viewed my work as interesting, they believed it was a project that would never come to fruition.

I had a nightmare the night before our meeting that Dr. Jansen recommended that I be dismissed from the university immediately. My pounding heart woke me up and reminded me that it was just a dream. Even though I was in a better headspace than I was a year before, a current of nervousness still ran through me.

As she acknowledged my chapter to be in decent shape, it was clear that Dr. Jansen was on board, and like me, had eyes on a Spring 2017 defense. We discussed the final benchmarks I needed to complete in the next six months. As we wrapped up, Dr. Jansen said, with a smile, "Vanessa, by hook or by crook, we will get there!" She offered the validation I was looking for: that she firmly believed that I could finish.

The following day, Dr. Jansen emailed me with a concrete deadline of when to submit my first complete draft of the dissertation: December 20th. I wrote back that it would be a race to get there, but manageable. She enthusiastically replied, "Let's do this!" It finally felt like a team effort.

The momentum kept fueling my productivity. I sent my first two chapters ahead to Dr. Davis, the first reader on my dissertation committee. Although she had a series of suggested revisions, she noted that they were "very good chapters" - more affirmation.

It was the week where things were finally coming together. Operation Endgame was fully in place, and I tackled the remaining writing with anticipation, not dread.

***

Writing often felt like a selfish endeavor. My research about medieval devotional practices did not feel like it offered a meaningful contribution to the world. During my final academic year of graduate school, I signed up to be a coach for a local Girls on the Run team. Volunteering with this organization became one of the most rewarding experiences of my life. Girls on the Run is a non-profit program that encourages young girls to develop a positive self-image and healthy lifestyle through both interactive lessons and running games. This 12-week program, filled with a rich curriculum, culminates in a celebratory 5k run with 1,000 girls from all eight wards in D.C.

Although I had nearly a decade of experience working with kids at CTY, this was the first time I had worked with students who were between eight- and ten-years-old. I was unaccustomed to saying things like, "Stephanie, stop picking up the grass," "Katie, keep your hands to yourself," and most commonly, "Please cover your mouth when you cough or sneeze (and not do it in my face)!" Despite these little things, the girls were so fun to interact with, and their enthusiasm was contagious. Their excitement over the little things: stickers to put on their achievement charts, running games we played on the grassy lawn, and running through the National Zoo, made going to practice a refreshing break from the quiet and monotonous world of writing. My mind couldn't drift to the to-do list that awaited me after practice. Rather, it was my responsibility to keep them safe, engage them in our lessons, and be fully present in all of our activities.

A few hours before I headed to practice on November 8, 2016, I had spent the morning phone banking at the Woman's National Democratic Club, thrilled to be helping in some small way on what promised to be a historical night. wearing a shirt that said, "Run like a girl" with a picture of the White House, I was excited to call people to remind them that it was Election Day and how they could find their polling stations. That exuberance and optimism gave way to sobbing and dread as the exit polls came in, as I worried what this meant for the future of our country.

In her gracious concession speech, Hillary Clinton addressed an important demographic, "To all the little girls who are watching this, never doubt that you are valuable and powerful and deserving of every chance and opportunity in the world to pursue and achieve your own dreams." In the wake of the 2016 election, I was more motivated than ever to work with these girls, whose entire future lay before them. I wanted them to know that an adult cared about their self-worth and ability to make a difference in the world.

***

Like many, I cried for days after the 2016 election. I called my mom, who tried to assure me things wouldn't be as bad as I feared (when in actuality, things became much worse than we predicted). "Are you working on your chapter?" Mom asked. "Couldn't that be a good way to keep your mind off of things?" I told her, "I can't – I keep crying whenever I try to write."

"Vanessa, you need to keep going. You want to finish and you're so close. You can't let this get in the way of you finishing." My mom was right - even though my desire to work was minimal, I could not let this horrible political catastrophe throw a wrench in the momentum I had been building all semester.

When it was time to make dinner two days after the election, I was more than ready to put aside my work for the evening. I was going to make what I recently learned was Pat's favorite childhood dinner: grilled cheese and tomato soup. After knocking out the first few steps for the soup, I needed to purée the tomatoes. I wished I had accepted my mother's offer to buy me an immersion blender. I foolishly decided that a good alternative was to, in small batches, blend the tomatoes in the blender we received as a wedding gift.

I poured two cups of tomatoes in the blender, and with my hand firmly placed on top, pressed "purée." The sheer volume of the tomatoes, coupled with the high-speed setting, blew the lid right off. "NO!" I screamed, as I frantically hit the "off" button. It was too late. The kitchen immediately turned into a culinary crime scene, with some of the tomatoes even reaching the ceiling. I was drenched head-to-toe in the gooey mess, and burst into tears. The world was already falling apart, and now, I was wearing the dinner that was meant to offer Pat an iota of comfort in the post-election nightmare.

What I should've done was get out of my clothes, jump in the shower, and order take-out. Instead, I stood rooted to the spot, weeping - everything felt like a disaster. Suddenly, Pat walked in, looking horrified as he saw his wife, looking not like Donna Reid, but a twisted cross between Lucille Ball and the end of *Carrie*. "What happened?" he asked. "I wanted to make you (sniff sniff), something nice," I said between sobs, bits of tomato dripping off my clothes.

One of Pat's strengths is his ability to dive into action, especially when I find myself in any predicament. "Don't move," he said, quickly changing into an old t-shirt and shorts. He helped me change out of the stained clothes, immediately throwing them into the washing machine. He handed me my bathrobe, "Take a shower, I'll clean things up."

By the time I got out of the bathroom, the ceiling had returned to its usual shade of white, and Pat was tackling the mess on the floor.

The world remained terrible. No amount of tomato soup (or eventually, the Chinese food Pat ordered) changed the results of the election. But in that moment, my failed attempt at an act of generosity elicited a wonderful act of kindness from the person I leaned on the most.

***

That fall, I was putting together my final chapter. While most of my chapters had their origins in the dissertation proposal I had written three years before, I needed to do extensive research on textual narratives that imagined Mary's mournful response at the Crucifixion. I had found a series of compelling representations of Mary's mourning that varied from inarticulate sobs to eloquent speech enabled Mary to convey her unbounded grief. I compared these stories with medieval accounts about female mourning that described women who were prone to "loud and violent sobbing, shouting, screaming, and even falling over and writhing on the ground." In many cases, Mary appeared to be the model mourner, and was held up as a figure for medieval women to imitate. I was less familiar with this topic, and hadn't had the time to bounce these ideas around with my classmates and professors. Sending in the chapter shortly before Thanksgiving, I hoped that it would be up to Dr. Jansen's satisfaction.

After she read that chapter, Dr. Jansen wrote, "I'm beginning to see light at the end of the tunnel." I had finally received enough encouraging feedback to feel galvanized and energized for the homestretch of 2016. I threw everything I had to make sure that the full draft was ready for submission. This process resurfaced a memory from the early stages of the writing process.

Back in 2012, when, a few months into my research, I had discovered someone else's dissertation on "the vengeful Virgin Mary" - a topic too similar to the one I was considering, Dr. Jansen told me that the initial research that I had already done would "not be in vain." At that moment, I didn't have the perspective to truly believe her. It wasn't until the end of 2016, when I was trying to tie everything together in my introduction, I returned to some of the free writing I had done in 2012. Even though it needed polishing, some of the old writing from nearly five years before found a home in the final version of the dissertation. "Not in vain" was right. Both writing a dissertation and running required years of cumulative effort, and the work done on any given day was part of the bricklaying that enabled me to climb my way to victory. During that monster month, I also spent most of my evenings and weekends writing and revising. Although it was exhausting, it was also exciting.

I had recently finished reading Shonda Rhimes's memoir, *Year of Yes: How to Dance It Out, Stand in the Sun and Be Your Own Person*. Shonda wrote about the best moments of her writing process, which she referred to as "the hum,"

"A hum begins in my brain and it grows and it grows and that hum sounds like the open road and I could drive it forever… The hum is action and activity, the hum is a drug, the hum is music, the hum is light and air, the hum is God's whisper right in my ear."

I instantly understood this. When I've had amazing races, and I've been able to lock in without distraction or falling off the pace, I've felt the hum. When I've been able to sit with my laptop for extended periods of time, with a sense of single-minded determination, that's the hum. In this home stretch of the dissertation, my mind regularly vibrated on a higher frequency than it ever had. The hum was real.

On December 20th, I proudly submitted a complete draft of my dissertation. To see the whole process come together, to print out and bind a full draft of 315 pages that could be read from cover to cover, brought back the feeling of satisfaction that came with doing my first 20-mile run nearly eight years before. Both events were met with fatigue, as well as a sense of accomplishment and excitement for what the major milestone meant for the future.

When I turned in my full draft, Dr. Jansen gave a recommendation that differed from her usual comments:

Once you submit this, do not look at it for several weeks. Give yourself permission to set this aside. At this point, you're so close to the project that you now need to create some distance between you and it. Don't think about it over the holidays. That way, when I give you feedback in January, you're looking at your writing with fresh eyes.

I happily put my laptop away and geared up for the holiday season, eager for a break.

Chapter 14: The Finish Line

"I have fought the good fight. I have completed the
race. I have kept the faith." – 2 Timothy 4:7

I didn't touch the dissertation for three weeks. Pat and
I went on a weeklong vacation to St. Michaels: a small coastal
town on the Chesapeake Bay. We relaxed as we celebrated Christmas – our first real vacation since our honeymoon over two
years before. One day, Pat treated me to a massage, and as the
masseuse worked on my shoulders, I felt the years of accumulated tension leaving my body.

As we lounged in our ocean-themed suite at the Harbour
Inn, I happily buried my nose in my pleasure books. It was wonderful to enjoy reading after months of intensively scrutinizing
my own writing. This was a sharp contrast from the majority
of grad school, when I had opted to withhold one of my favorite hobbies as "incentive" to work on my dissertation. Looking
back, I regret doing that. I knew many marathoners who gave up
some sort of indulgence during their training, such as ice cream
or alcohol. But in giving up something that they could enjoy in
moderation, such as a glass of wine at the end of the day, they
lost the ability to enjoy a minor indulgence or reward that came
from their hard work. Once I realized I didn't have to punish myself with a restricted lifestyle, I could enjoy my hobbies, and then
return to the task at hand.

On New Year's Eve, we went out to dinner at a nearby inn.
We were seated in oversized chairs by an enormous fireplace and
could hear the jazz quartet playing swing music in the nearby
ballroom. As we sipped cocktails, we discussed our resolutions
for 2017. I felt more optimistic about my goals; namely, success-

fully defending my dissertation, than I had in any of the other New Year's we had celebrated together. We clinked our glasses, excited to be getting closer to the next phase of our lives.

***

For years, the dissertation was a dark cloud that hovered over me. My anxiety enlarged the cloud – it was part of the imposter syndrome that had afflicted me throughout graduate school. But at the end of 2016, the cloud started to shrink. Part of it was the positive feedback I was receiving, and another part was the realization that the dream was truly becoming a reality.

I knew the cloud had shrunk when I gave a paper at an academic conference in early January 2017. Many of the participants asked about my dissertation, and for once, a knot did not form in my stomach. Nor were my words carefully crafted, told with a forced smile and feigned optimism. Instead, I could feel the genuine optimism and excitement as I updated any inquirers, "Yes, I turned in a full draft!" "It looks like if everything goes right, I'll defend in the spring!"

***

When the first round of feedback arrived in January 2017, I tackled Dr. Jansen's comments with enthusiasm. There was a newfound intensity to my work, which sustained me during those final months of graduate school.

Amid my revisions, I coached Girls on the Run, taught my Crusades course at the University of Maryland, and submitted job applications in the hopes of finding gainful employment. Each day was filled with some course prep, a few hours of revisions, job applications, and some running. I finally learned how to balance my workload. I prided myself on the fact that I never pulled an all-nighter in the entirety of my education: not in high school, college, or grad school. It became part of my philosophy to train and write smarter, not harder. It was a lesson that I only came to truly appreciate after years of burning the candle at both ends.

At the end of January, Dr. Jansen gave me her blessing to submit the revised version to my committee. I asked her with some trepidation, "Does this mean my parents can buy their plane tickets for commencement?" Swatting me on the arm, she chided, "Vanessa – of course you are graduating!" I responded, half-indignantly, "Well, I thought I was moving in that direction, but I needed to hear you say the words!" I had known classmates who thought they would graduate in a particular semester, only to be confronted with the inevitable disappointment of a setback. It was such a relief to know that things were finally going according to plan.

Less than a week later, Dr. Davis sent in her own set of comments. Because I could see the timestamps on Track Changes in Microsoft Word, it appeared as if she reviewed my dissertation for two days straight. To say Dr. Davis was thorough was an understatement. She asked questions such as "What is the semantic range of this word at the time?" and "Any sense of this as an Old Testament practice?" In total, it was 729 comments. Some comments took minutes to address: others required extensive thinking and revising for hours on end. I knew the time spent working on this feedback continued to make the dissertation a better piece of scholarship. Those final months of revisions were some of the happiest moments of graduate school.

***

April 4, 2017

I am defending my dissertation on April 12th. I've written, edited, revised, thrown out the bad parts, and had it vetted by my committee. Just like I visualized my races, I also did this leading up to my defense. I have visited the room in advance, I know what outfit I'll wear, and I've planned a schedule for my defense day. I've tried to imagine the kinds of questions my professors will ask and have brainstormed potential answers that I can readily rattle off.

The dream I've had of getting my doctorate since the first semester of my freshman year at Holy Cross is about to become a reality. Decades of a life-long education are concluding before my eyes. Yes, I know, those who love to learn never stop learning. But the daily rigors of school: writing, studying, meeting with professors, all of that is almost over.

On Tuesday, I had my last meeting with Dr. Jansen before the defense. We chatted about what to prepare for and things to think about in the coming weeks. She asked how I was feeling, now that I had submitted the written product. "To be honest," I responded, "It may not be polite to say, but I feel pretty good." The department does not let you defend until they are truly convinced that you're ready. They put all of these hurdles up, and if you can get over them without knocking them down, it's game time. The two hours of the defense will be challenging, and I anticipate some butterflies, but I'm also excited for the big day.

***

In the marathon, the race always manifested itself as a victory lap: an endurance challenge and celebration after months of hard work. Dr. Jansen described the defense (a two-hour oral examination with six professors) similarly. She said it was an opportunity for a great discussion, and that I should enjoy the fact that six people had carefully read my dissertation. How could a two-hour test be pleasant? Surely, she had forgotten her own defense.

In the week leading up to the defense, I remained calm. I crafted my twenty-minute opening statement, and rehearsed it repeatedly. I even silently practiced it on my runs, as if recreating the mind-body magic of my "Swim to Modernity" exercise from when I took my comprehensive exams. Over the phone, my mom heard me recite my introduction every day for a week. She had patiently helped me for the SATs, comps, and now, she had a front-row seat to my last final exam ever.

The day before the defense, I went for a run, listening to my favorite pump-up music, which included Katy Perry's Olympic song "Rise,"

> *Oh, ye of so little faith*
> *Don't doubt it, don't doubt it*
> *Victory is in my veins*
> *I know it, I know it*

And I will not negotiate
I'll fight it, I'll fight it
I will transform

Although it was 75 degrees out, I got chills as I listened to the lyrics on my run. It was a strange sensation to get goosebumps while sweating. I knew something special was about to happen. I was focused, I was excited, and I was ready.

That confidence vanished when it was time for bed. It was as if someone flipped a switch in my head. My heart raced and I tossed and turned all night: a terrible return to the sleepless nights that had plagued much of my experience as a grad student.

The next morning, I set out for a run, hoping that hitting the pavement would do its usual trick of eliminating my pent-up nerves. Not on Defense Day. Five miles is a long time to run while anxious, and my heart pounded in my chest. Even though the pace was easy, my chest was tight and my breathing felt constricted. It wasn't until I was a few blocks from home that the knot in my stomach and shortness of breath finally disappeared. Looking to stay relaxed before leaving home, I put on an episode of "Golden Girls." The goofy antics of the show kept me calm as I got dressed. Pat kissed me goodbye, "You'll be great, and I can't wait to celebrate with you afterwards. You've got this."

I got to campus early, which gave me some quiet time to myself, including at the chapel of Our Lady of Perpetual Help. That chapel had provided peace before Latin exams, comps, and now my dissertation defense. After a few final moments of prayer, I headed to the conference room for my exam, arriving at the same time as Dr. Jansen.

"Breathe. Relax," she encouraged. I smiled and tried to not belie the confidence I was trying to project. She asked if I wanted coffee - I politely declined. I didn't need to feel more jittery. The other professors slowly trickled in: Dr. Paxton, Dr. Sherman, and via Skype, Dr. Davis, who was away on sabbatical, and the two external reviewers. They chatted amongst themselves as I sought to keep my mind clear, and let their conversation wash over me.

Once I began to speak, my nerves finally faded for good. As I laid out the parameters of my dissertation, it felt as routine and rhythmic as a regular run. While I spoke, I tried to make eye contact with each professor. As I caught Dr. Jansen's eye, I expected her to have a serious, focused expression on her face, similar to the one I had seen in countless classes and lectures with her since I started at CUA in 2008. Instead, she was smiling.

Relief flooded through my body. *Oh, this is going to be okay.* Dr. Jansen had known me since I was a brand-new, wide-eyed graduate student when I arrived at CUA at 22 years old. My dissertation defense reflected on her as much as it did on me. I tucked away that warm feeling and continued to speak until I received my cue to wrap up my opening statement.

The second part of the defense consisted of each professor asking a series of questions in 15-minute increments. Before Dr. Jansen launched into her first question, she opened by saying; "First of all, Vanessa, I want to commend you on this project. In your exploration of Mary's voice, you introduced us to this fascinating topic..." More relief. *Everyone is on board. This is finally going to happen. You are about to achieve what you've worked toward your entire life.*

All of those years of coursework and studying came together on that day, similar to the years of training propelled me to success at the Boston Marathon. I knew how to address the questions my professors asked and how to precisely explain my methodology. Equally as important, I also knew how to get myself to the defense mentally ready.

Even while I was speaking, I was aware of the fact that through the process of writing a dissertation about the importance of a historical woman's voice, I found my own voice. I spent much of my graduate career trying to prove to both others and myself that I deserved a seat at the table. I had spent years writing about women's agency and power, and because women like Dr. Jansen and Dr. Davis chose to empower me, I was able to grow and develop as a historian.

After the last question, I was sent into the hall for them to deliberate. Six people held the fate of my professional future in their hands. Dr. Jansen said, "Go for a walk - it'll be a few minutes. We have to talk and then fill out some paperwork."

Dr. Jansen and the rest of the committee wouldn't have scheduled the defense if they thought I would fail. Failure would be a reflection on the entire department. I knew that there was a reception scheduled in my honor in about 20 minutes - they wouldn't have ordered cake and champagne if they thought the defense would be a bust. Until the door opened, I wouldn't believe it. *Tick tock. Tick tock.*

Finally, the door opened, and Dr. Jansen walked out with a big smile, uttering the words I'd been longing to hear since my first year at Holy Cross: "Congratulations, Dr. Corcoran."

It was all over. All of those years of classes, reading, writing, studying, and worrying I'd ever finish, finally materialized into a dream come true. At my reception, I happily chatted with my professors and classmates who had supported me throughout the journey, while Pat stood next to me, proud and relieved to see me reach this milestone at last.

I managed to finish right ahead of the university's deadline of May 2017, despite a few statistics that loomed in my mind. I knew only about 57 percent of doctoral students earn their Ph.D. within 10 years of starting. I also knew that the average student takes 8.2 years to slog through a Ph.D. program and is 33 years old before earning that top diploma. It took me seven years, and I was scheduled to graduate at age 30.

After we polished off the champagne, Pat headed back to work and I walked toward the metro to go home. I was exhausted and couldn't wait to unwind. While for the train to arrive, I grabbed my phone to check my email. Dr. Davis, who monitored my defense via Skype, had written to me: "Congratulations, both for the interesting, compelling research you did and your defense of it. I was reflecting on how much you have grown since coming to CUA. I'm very proud of you and I hope you are proud of yourself."

Dr. Davis was the one who encouraged me in 2011 to pursue the dissertation topic that inspired me. She had challenged me in my thinking and her continual dedication throughout the process helped me to grow as a scholar when I needed it the most.

I was told that after the defense, professors often hand a series of edits to the student that must be addressed before they can officially finish. As I rode the train home that afternoon, I realized my professors hadn't mandated any more revisions. There was nothing to change. I was truly done. Ignoring the other commuters on the train, I put my head in my hands and cried tears of joy.

Chapter 15: Beyond the Race

"There is no finish line." – Joan Benoit Samuelson,
1984 Olympic Marathon Champion

A couple of weeks after my defense, the history department treated its faculty and students to a happy hour at Busboys and Poets, one of the favorite CUA hangouts in Brookland. As some of the students shared stories about some of their bouts of nervousness in grad school, I revealed to Dr. Jansen that I had a recurring fear that she was going to throw me out of the program.

She initially laughed. However, as I relayed one of the anecdotes that had convinced me of my impending failure, Dr. Jansen's face fell. She exclaimed, "Vanessa, that's ridiculous! I can't believe you thought that. If you ever said that to me, I would've told you that your status here wasn't in jeopardy. We all believed in you." My head games were often my greatest obstacle to overcome, and this episode was once again proof that I was my own worst critic.

***

With the weight of the defense off my chest, I was able to fully enjoy the little things, like taking Heshie for a walk, going out to dinner with Pat, and coaching Girls on the Run. Because of the proximity of the girls' school in Northwest Washington, we often took them on runs through Rock Creek Park. But on special days, we loved surprising them with routes that cut through the National Zoo – which happened to be a few blocks away from their school. The girls loved passing by the giraffes and pandas on their run and often conveniently paused to stretch in front of their favorite animals.

As the weather warmed up in Washington, the zoo set up small misting stations for visitors, and the girls loved running through them to cool off. They chatted nonstop as they ran, and often yelled in excitement when things caught their attention. One day, they cried out, "Look, Coach Vanessa – a rainbow!" The misting station had created a small rainbow, and the girls ran over to it with unbridled delight. Having eliminated the stress of graduate school, smaller moments like this became more magnified in their ability to bring joy.

***

A month after my defense, my whole family arrived for Commencement. Time and time again, my family encouraged me to hope and dream, and equally as important, when they saw that my confidence wavered, they reminded me that they knew I could do this. My sibling Nova came in from Brooklyn, and I was grateful that they were able to make the trip. My parents, and more notably, my grandparents, have attended every single graduation of mine, from preschool to the conferral of my doctoral degree, which was complete with all of the accouterments of academic regalia. I know they were all proud of me, but this ceremony carried particular significance for my grandma.

My grandma, Lucille McGuire, has always had a special devotion to the Virgin Mary. Needless to say, she was beyond thrilled that I had chosen to write my dissertation about the woman she often referred to as "her favorite lady." Lucille regularly asked about the specifics of my research, and reportedly told everyone in their neighborhood, "My granddaughter is writing a book on the Blessed Virgin Mother, and you *know* how much I love Mary." I was proud to present her with her own bound copy at graduation. While I knew she would eventually read the whole thing (impressively, she finished it a few months later), I made sure she turned to the dedication page, which read,

This dissertation is lovingly dedicated to my grandmother, Lucille McGuire, for immeasurable reasons, and because Mary is "her favorite lady."

She beamed. It was the highlight of graduation weekend.

***

While Commencement was a wonderful day, there was a tinge of regret knowing that I did not have a job lined up. Honestly, I thought I would graduate with a job offer in hand. In fact, I was so confident that I'd find gainful employment early on, that I worried how I would balance beginning a new job during the final months of writing my dissertation. But when I received my diploma on May 13, 2017, I had no major leads.

It wasn't arrogance that had pushed me to thinking that I would quickly find a job. My professors often said, "Vanessa, you've got many skills to offer, of course someone is going to hire you!" With that encouragement, I set off writing cover letters and formatting resumes. I kept stumbling on job openings in academic advising, colleges' honors programs, and other areas of academic support, that made me think, "That would be an *amazing* job!" After submitting my application, the waiting game commenced. Once again, I was filled with that same mixture of dread and excitement that came over me whenever I turned in a dissertation chapter.

Usually at an inopportune time, such as ten minutes before teaching, a rejection email appeared in my inbox. I tried to collect myself and get ready to deliver my lecture on the Crusades. Teaching turned my mind off. However, when the class ended, reality set back in. Was I going to be the unemployed Ph.D.?

I couldn't get that term out of my head – "the unemployed Ph.D." My parents, professors, everyone quickly corrected me and tell me that I wasn't unemployed – I was "in transition." Semantics, really. Because it didn't feel great to receive the same question time and time again, "so, do you have a job lined up?"

With teeth clenched and a fake smile plastered on my face, I'd respond with a little speech I had rehearsed, "I prioritized finishing my dissertation over job searching. It wasn't until a few months ago that I started applying for jobs and I'm really happy with that choice. After all, it meant I was able to graduate on time." Saying that brought back all those stomach-churning feelings of when people innocently asked, "So, when do you think you'll be finished?"

I felt worn down. I had applied to dozens of jobs, and rarely did I even get offered an opportunity to interview. I had equated employment with a sense of self-worth, and the lack of offers made me feel inadequate. Frustrated after getting yet another rejection letter, I wrote to Dr. Davis, expressing my disappointment. She responded with some encouragement and perspective,

There are a number of "negative resumes" floating around these days, which are a record of all the things someone has applied for and not gotten. These are inevitably a lot longer than one's actual resume. You have a lot of skills and talents to offer and you will find a job that suits them. It may take longer than one would like. So, my advice is to be persistent and to reward yourself for the steps along the way.

I held onto this advice and returned to her words whenever I needed to remember that there was still reason to be optimistic.

In the middle of July, I interviewed for a job at CUA to be the Assistant Director of Tutoring Services. I woke up early for a sunrise run, and headed to campus listening to the same pump-up music that got me ready to go for my dissertation defense. After surviving my dissertation defense, I knew I could endure three hour-long interviews talking about my previous work experiences. The following day, I was delighted to receive a job offer, which I happily accepted. In total, I had applied to 37 jobs. The persistence, the networking, and most importantly, the willingness to keep applying, finally paid off.

***

I was back at CUA - the institution where I had spent the last nine years as a student. Although I now had a full-time job, some things hadn't changed. My office was in the same library where I had spent so many hours studying and writing. Even though I was finally more put-together than the young woman who smacked her head on the door on the first day of grad school, it felt hard to get my now-colleagues to look at me as a professional and not the 22-year-old they had met nearly a decade before.

Once I learned the ropes of my new position and made it through the first few months of the job, I realized that I wasn't finding the satisfaction I had hoped would be a part of my professional life. I had chased one singular goal for my entire adult life, and now that I had earned my doctorate, I wasn't sure what was left to accomplish. I wasn't getting challenged on a regular basis, and the hands-off approach my boss took meant that I ultimately worked in a vacuum. It felt nearly as isolating as the years spent writing my dissertation - an experience I was not interested in repeating. There was a clear lack of interest in my professional growth on my boss's part. My first performance review was fine, but not getting challenged left me feeling unfulfilled.

Was this what it meant to have a job? Just showing up, punching out, without feeling a meaningful connection to the work? Should I be complacent and coast through the next few years of work? Yet, having gone through an exhausting job search process less than a year before, I was reluctant to initiate another full-blown job hunt. Instead, I began to write the first draft of this book, hoping to find an outlet for my untapped creativity. On occasion, I applied for jobs that truly aligned with my professional interests and aspirations of moving into academic administration.

Many of the job descriptions spoke about the basic parameters typical for academic advising: student caseload, partnering with the counseling center and other student support offices. However, one advising position at Georgetown University also looked for candidates with an appreciation for the value of a liberal arts education and an understanding of Georgetown's Jesuit and Catholic identity. Having spent my undergrad years at Holy Cross, another Jesuit institution, I was eager for the chance to return to a university where the community shared my values.

Later that summer, I was invited to an on-campus interview. Not wanting to let my boss know I was interviewing for a job; I took a sick day. His communication with me had virtually ceased since the spring: my absence barely registered as a blip on his radar.

In a stark difference from the office dynamic at Catholic, where there was a lack of cohesiveness and collegiality, I watched as the three deans: Sue, Tad, and Marlene, playfully interact with each other - they had worked together for nearly two decades and seemed quite comfortable with each other. Even as we talked about topics such as Jesuit identity, commitment to pedagogy, and academic advising, I felt like I was speaking to people with whom I could easily connect. I wasn't nervous: only excited at the prospect of joining this office.

As if making the case for why I should consider the position, Sue leaned forward eagerly, and with a smile across her face said, "Most of us have been here between 10 to 20 years - there isn't a lot of turnaround. We've seen each other grow professionally, and we've also watched our colleagues get married and have children. Our office is a family. We think you'd be able to make a valuable contribution to our office and to our students." In that moment, I saw myself standing between two worlds: a job that lacked meaning, and the glimpse of not a job, but a vocation.

As the interview drew to a close, the deans started to ask specific questions that indicated that they were trying to evaluate my level of interest in the position. At that point, I said, "I'm going to be frank and put all of my cards on the table. I'm really interested in this position." They thanked me for my candor, and told me that they'd get in touch with me soon.

When they called to offer me the position a few days later, I accepted without a moment's hesitation. It was time to bid farewell to my time at Catholic, and move to a place that offered upward mobility and the sense that I was viewed as a respected colleague.

I enjoyed getting to know my new colleagues. They all seemed happy and invested in their work and each other. At lunch, our conversations drifted away from work and instead, often revolved around new books we were reading, family updates, and sometimes good stories that made my stomach hurt from laughing. I noticed that my happiness at work then enabled me to enjoy my home life more as well. Instead of feeling a sense of dread on Sunday evenings about the upcoming week, I felt happier and more satisfied than I ever had in my adult life.

Students came in to get guidance on their courses, potential career paths, and for advice on when they felt overwhelmed. These high-performing students frequently came to me when they received a bad grade on a test or paper. To them, their entire future was in jeopardy. The pressure from their families, the competitive nature they have with their peers, and the pressure they put on themselves to do well took an incredible toll on them. After I told them that no single assignment or grade will define them, I proceeded to tell them that I shared those precise concerns when I was in school. The first time a student visibly exhaled in my office and said, "I feel so much better now that I've talked with you," I knew I was exactly where I belonged.

***

It was quiet in the office during finals week at Georgetown. Listening to Christmas music while I answered emails, I was startled when the phone rang. It was our administrative assistant, "Your advisor is here to see you," she said. "I'm sorry, what?" I asked, completely confused. Through the phone, I heard that familiar Julia Child laughter that I instantly recognized as that of Dr. Jansen's. "Send her down!" I asked.

Kate, as I was now told to call her, was on campus to visit our dean: a fellow medievalist and old friend of hers. Knowing that my office was nearby, she decided to stop by to see how I was settling into my new job.

I watched as my mentor looked around my carefully-decorated office. She saw my framed diplomas, two of which were earned under her tutelage. Kate then glanced at my coat rack, upon which hung my academic regalia: the long black doctoral robe that was worn at formal academic occasions. As she sat down, her eyes traveled to my bookshelves, which contained all of the books I had amassed in graduate school, as well as a series of pictures of me and Pat: a relationship that grew from an eHarmony date into a marriage during my dissertation years.

A flood of memories came back. For years, whenever I sat outside of Dr. Jansen's office, waiting for her, I could feel my stomach churning as I worried about our conversation. Once invited inside, I sat in the guest chair across from her desk as we discussed my writing. My shoulders tensed up as I hunched over my notebook, trying to frantically write down all of her advice.

But on this day, Kate occupied the guest chair, and I felt completely relaxed. I had nothing more to prove to her. Instead, we caught up like old colleagues. I happily spoke about my new job, and my excitement about the history seminar on the Virgin Mary that I planned to teach the following semester. Taking off her glasses, as if to underscore a point, she said, "You've really carved out a wonderful path for yourself, Vanessa, and I couldn't be happier for you." I didn't need her blessing, but her words affirmed my own sense of fulfilment about my new life.

When I graduated from Holy Cross in 2008, I wrote in my Purple Journal about my dream of my future life, "I hope my students want to be in my classes and to come to my office for guidance and assistance. I imagine an office full of books, images, and objects that are all indicative of my love for the Middle Ages." The dream that was first inspired over a decade before had at last crystallized into a reality.

When I arrived in D.C. in 2008 with my knees shaking and voice quavering, I couldn't have foreseen what life had in store for me. Equally as big as my dreams was the fear that despite my best efforts, I was inadequate compared to my peers. It took years to learn how to turn down that negative self-talk and replace it with an inner monologue that instilled confidence. As I realized that the training methods that I used to become a successful runner were transformational, running became more than a confidence booster. I began to use these running and mental techniques both on and off the road. Earning my Ph.D.

did not erase my doubts of inadequacy completely, but the sense of accomplishment gave me a feeling of self-assurance that I had been seeking.

At last, I had accomplished what I wanted professionally. It was now time to do what I had delayed for so long - have a baby.

Chapter 16: Pregnancy and the Pandemic

"With COVID-19, we've made it to the life raft. Dry land is far away." – Marc Lipsitch, epidemiologist, March 2020

Even before Pat and I got married in 2014, we knew we wanted to have a baby, but thought it would be best to wait until after I was done with school. I wanted to be able to fully enjoy being a parent and not spend the first few years of motherhood spent hunched over the computer while I was trying to finish my dissertation. After I graduated, I wanted to get settled into my new career. In the spring of 2019, I finally felt like I was in a good place at Georgetown. I trained for my first marathon in eight years, wanting to do one more race before I tried to get pregnant. Satisfied with my finishing time of 3:33, I went off the pill and waited for my period to come back.

Even though people told me I needed to be patient, it was hard to wait and let nature take its course. I had my ovulation sticks, a fertility app, and pregnancy tests all ready. As we shifted into summer and no positive tests emerged, I hoped a summer vacation would do the trick. Nothing. "It's really early," Pat said gently. "I know you would will this baby into existence if you could, but it's going to take some time." Knowing that one of the complications of Celiac Disease is infertility, I worried that I'd have a hard time getting pregnant.

I tried to distract myself with house hunting. With a baby hopefully on the horizon and two steady incomes, I was eager for us to move out of our studio apartment and find our forever home where we could raise a family. Whenever we took a tour, the house's realtor asked if we had any kids. It pained me to say, "No, but hopefully soon."

At the end of August, we got together with Pat's family to celebrate his father's 70th birthday. His brother Jack was there, and I knew that he and his wife had been trying to have a baby as well. I told Pat, "They're going to announce at this gathering that they're pregnant, and we just need to be prepared for that." No announcement came. A few days later, Jack texted us a picture of an ultrasound. The picture was a gut punch, and as I looked at it, tears streamed down my face. Pat hugged me as I cried. Watching someone else get their happy moment while we were waiting for ours was hard.

One day in early October, I was dealing with some difficult student cases at work, including one who needed to go on a medical leave due to clinical depression, and I felt frazzled. I texted Pat: "Not having a great day." By the time he came home, I was in tears. After a few minutes of gently rubbing my back, Pat cautiously asked, "Could you be pregnant? Maybe it's hormonal." I went to my bag of pregnancy tests - I had taken so many before that ended in disappointment. This time, thin pink lines appeared. But knowing that I was only a few weeks pregnant made me hesitant to get excited this soon. "I think we're pregnant," I told Pat, my voice couched with hesitation as I showed him the test. Pat must've taken his cues from me, because though he seemed happy, I don't think he was entirely confident that it was a reality. I tried to sleep that night but my head was buzzing with a mixture of nervousness and excitement. In the coming days, other some mood swings (which could've been attributed to a variety of things), I didn't feel pregnant.

A week later, exhaustion set in. I started to believe that the pregnancy was real, but we were also in the process of moving into our new house - that could also be the reason for the exhaustion. I felt like I was walking on eggshells - afraid to do anything that could hurt the baby.

Two days after we moved into our new house, we had our first OB appointment at Georgetown Hospital. I was nervous - what if the doctor couldn't see a heartbeat on the ultrasound?

My knees were shaking in the stirrups. While gripping Pat's hand, I waited as the doctor carefully positioned the ultrasound wand on my stomach. A static black and white blur appeared before us. "There's the..." the doctor started. There was no mistaking what she was pointing to - I could see our baby. Sheer relief flooded through me. This baby was real and although it was the size of a blueberry, it was a healthy little baby. Pat squeezed my hand - he was relieved too. The dream started to feel more real, and I tightly clutched that sonogram picture, sneaking a peak at it at work every chance I got.

The night after my sonogram, I asked my parents if we could FaceTime, under the auspices of showing them our new house. We chatted for a few minutes, and I told them that while there were a lot of boxes and clutter, maybe they'd want to see this instead. I held up the sonogram.

Utter surprise and joy chased across their faces as they looked at the picture. My mom started bawling and my dad said it was one of the happiest days of his life. They had no greater joy in the world than being parents, and now they were going to have their first grandchild. I had always imagined this moment would be full of hugs, but it was done over FaceTime. In no way could we ever expect that so much of what was to come with our new baby would be done virtually.

I continued to run during my first trimester, but even a three-mile run left me exhausted. Just as the pregnancy books said, once the first trimester ended, the all-encompassing fatigue lifted. My appetite returned and I felt like I had more energy. I was able to run further, and even though my average pace had slowed down from eight-minute-miles to ten-minute miles, I was happy to be able to continue running, knowing that it was good for both me and the baby.

I started to keep a baby journal, writing to document the pregnancy. Even though it felt odd to write letters to our unborn child, I hoped they would serve as a way for me to start connecting with them, and that later on, they could read the letters and learn what life was like when they were first born.

***

October 30, 2019

Dear baby,

It wasn't until I saw you on the ultrasound last week that I really believed that you were real. Our doctor wasn't sure if you'd appear on the ultrasound, but voila! You were there, clear as anything.

We've wanted you for so long. I was starting to wonder and worry if we'd ever get a baby. We know you are the answer to our prayers. We can't wait to meet you, sweet baby.

***

A few days before Thanksgiving, we got the results of the genetic screening: we were overjoyed to find out we were having a healthy baby girl. Relieved that this was on track to be a healthy pregnancy, we started telling our extended family about the baby. We had so much to be thankful for, and could not wait to share this news with our loved ones.

Even though there were many decisions we had to make before our daughter was born, one of the easiest, surprisingly, was choosing her name. I was grateful that Pat and I had the same idea – to honor my grandma by naming our daughter after her. While her full name would be Lucia, we would call her Lucy. We decided to tell everyone our daughter's name ahead of her birth, which made her feel all the more real. We were excited to meet baby Lucy, and happily started to make plans for her arrival.

I was looking forward to my baby shower, because it would give me a chance to see my family and friends before Lucy was born. My mom, so excited about becoming a grandmother, happily planned a small gathering for us in Rochester scheduled for March 21, 2020. At my 30-week check-up on March 6th, I asked the OB if she had any concerns about me traveling to Rochester, given that a new airborne disease called coronavirus was starting to spread, especially on the West Coast. "I'll wear a mask on the plane," I assured my doctor. "You'll be fine," she said. "Things don't seem to be too bad here on the East Coast."

On March 8th, Pat and I took a tour of the hospital and attended our first parenting class. As we walked around, looking at the different pieces of equipment and trying to assess whether the delivery rooms looked comfortable, it was hard to imagine what labor would be like. After the tour ended, we all sat around a table with baby dolls to practice diaper changes, swaddling, and infant CPR.

That parenting class turned out to be our last social outing. A few days later, the World Health Organization declared COVID-19 to be a pandemic. It felt like a slow-moving avalanche as things began to shut down. The next day, my office told us all to go home and plan to work remotely for a few weeks. With this announcement, I called my mom, "I think we need to cancel the baby shower," I told her. "This doesn't seem like a good idea." I had a lump in my throat as we talked, because I, along with the rest of the world, had no idea when I'd see my loved ones again.

My family threw me a virtual shower instead, as we all sat on FaceTime, as my mom, grandma, and aunts shared stories about their own babies. Kathleen had a cake delivered to my house, and it was the beginning of the outpouring of support I felt from a distance. My office followed suit, sending gifts and cupcakes and a card that said, "We can't wait to meet Lucy."

Our dreams had to adapt for the rapidly-changing world. I was watching the end of my pre-baby life slowly end, not with baby showers and fun last hurrah outings, but Zoom gatherings and phone calls. Although I had already anticipated that those early months of motherhood would be isolating, this was a heightened version of seclusion.

For years, I had imagined that along with Pat, my parents would be there for the arrival of their grandchild, and that nearby friends would see the baby. There was a terrible week at the end of March when the surge peaked New York City that women were not allowed to have their significant others with them in the delivery room. When Pat (who was still physically working in his office, as his office in the State Department was dealing with providing pandemic medical support to diplomats abroad) came home, I told him that this was happening, and that I was concerned it would happen for us, too. His face fell. Would he have to watch the birth of his first child over FaceTime? Thankfully, the uproar around this strict policy quickly caused a series of regulations to permit partners in the delivery room. This episode, so like many moments in March 2020, reaffirmed that Lucy's arrival would not look like we expected.

***

I continued to run every other day, finding it to be a good release from the stress of the pandemic and ever-changing news about how to protect ourselves from this aggressive virus. Even though I was eight months pregnant and slowed down to an 11-minute pace, it felt more fun to run than just walk.

One evening, just several blocks from my house, I lost my footing and hit the ground. I thankfully braced myself with my wrists to stop my pregnant belly from hitting the pavement. With blood streaming from my knees and elbows, I stood up, shaking, terrified.

I had worked so hard to protect Lucy through this pregnancy and a freaking pandemic - but did I just put my baby in danger? My mind went into catastrophic mode. What if the thing I love, running, was ultimately the thing that hurt, or even, God forbid, took away my baby?

I couldn't stop shaking as I staggered home and called Pat, and then the OB on call. I explained what happened, that I hadn't experienced any vaginal bleeding or contractions, and that Lucy kept kicking. The OB helped me to stay calm, "Vanessa, I know this is scary, but unless you fell directly on your stomach, babies have enough protective cushioning in utero to be fine after a fall. Keep monitoring, and call me if anything changes. I think you're fine."

For the next few hours, I felt so anxious. I got in the shower, washing the blood and dirt off of me. I stiffened up quickly as pain shot through my knees. As the water rinsed everything away, I started sobbing. I was incredibly scared.

Thankfully, Lucy kept kicking. Those baby taps, along with no signs of bleeding, kept me going all night.

I cautiously laid low, only going for short walks while my knees healed. It wasn't until my next OB appointment, when I heard that beautiful heartbeat and saw Lucy move across the monitor that I could truly breathe a sigh of relief. She was still safe. That afternoon, I cautiously laced up my sneakers and ran - scanning the ground for anything that could get in my way. Although it felt like my eyes were glued to the ground, I was happy to be able to return to running.

***

Even though my pace slowed considerably (and required more frequent bathroom stops), I was pleased that I could keep running through the end of pregnancy. Lucy kicked while I ran, happily moving around (an early indicator of what a spunky, active child she'd become). The running felt more like waddling as my belly grew, slowing down to 12-minute miles.

Lucy's due date (May 30th) was a few weeks after the semester ended. It was nice to wind down after a busy two months of remote advising. There were no signs that Lucy would arrive early. Pat and I relaxed throughout Memorial weekend - trying to enjoy the last few days of quiet. On Monday morning, I went out for a run. The oppressive D.C. heat hadn't hit yet, and the spring air felt refreshing. "Nice job, Mama!" cheered one pedestrian, my belly visible in my maternity running top. Even though my pace was slow, I ran five miles that morning – I felt peaceful and happy.

As we ate dinner that evening, Pat noticed that my pink shorts suddenly became darker. "Um...did you pee your pants or did your water just break?" Pat asked tentatively. Even though our kitchen floor was wet, I didn't feel any different: no contractions or movements. So, we packed our hospital bag and chatted with the OB on call, who said it was fine to take our time checking in. We took Heshie for a walk around the block, giving her one last hurrah before Lucy arrived.

Pat put on "Lucy in the Sky with Diamonds," in the car and we drove to the hospital. The admitting nurse looked at my driver's license, and noting my date of birth, croaked out in a raspy voice, "Ha, 1986, *that* was a great year." Already giddy, Pat and I tried to not burst out laughing. This joy set the tone for the next few hours as we got checked in.

I was already dilated at four centimeters, so it seemed like things were moving fast. Getting swabbed up the nose for my first Covid test while in labor was the most painful part of the process at that point. Though my face was masked, Pat could see my eyes water as I got swabbed - all admitted patients were tested for the virus. I was relieved when the test came back negative and everything could proceed as normal: at least as normal as giving birth during a pandemic could be.

The epidural kicked in and I felt good, bordering on euphoric. I happily chatted with all of the doctors and nurses. Pat was quick to tell them that I had just run five miles that morning, and they all thought I was in shape for a smooth delivery. Even as the contractions picked up, I made the mistake of telling Pat that I thought labor was "intuitive." After a few hours, I had dilated to ten centimeters, and the doctors and nurses said that I could start pushing, and at this rate, Lucy would arrive before sunrise.

"I can see her head!" Pat said excitedly. I sighed in relief - this was going by faster than I anticipated. But after a while, there was no further movement: it felt like she was stuck. One hour turned into two hours of pushing, and any thoughts I had of labor being "intuitive" had vanished. I could see a clock hanging on the wall, and it was hard to see how much time was passing without any sense of progress. At three hours, the doctor said, "If she doesn't come soon, we'll need to try to use the vacuum to get her out. If that doesn't work, we'll have to do a C-section." Ugh, these were not ideal options. I started to cry - I was exhausted and nothing was happening. Pat rubbed my head with a cool washcloth. No amount of encouragement seemed to work. I grabbed the basin next to my bed to throw up – the pain and exhaustion were too intense.

Four hours into pushing, the doctor said, "Ok, I think she's almost here. You need to do a couple of really strong pushes, and she'll be here. Can you do that?" Exhausted and with tears in my eyes, I nodded. "Let's do this." "Come on, Vanessa, Come on!" Pat was chanting for me like when he cheered me on at my races.

The moment I could feel Lucy leaving my body could only be described as thunderous - I could feel her passing through me and into the world. As Lucy made her first mighty cry into the world at 8:35 a.m. on May 26th, the doctors cleaned her up and put her on my chest. "You did it, you did it," cried Pat. At last, we had our baby girl, and she was perfect. She had dark hair, and weighing 6 pounds, 5 ounces, felt so small in my arms. Because no outside visitors were allowed because of Covid, we FaceTimed with our families - holding up our tiny little girl for them to see.

Our world changed in an instant. When we left the hospital two days later, it was scary to leave behind the team of doctors and nurses who were helping us learn how to be parents. And in the isolation of the pandemic, it became up to only me and Pat to protect Lucy from the virus ravaging the country. Becoming a new parent was daunting enough. The pandemic escalated that fear to a new level.

Chapter 17: Waiting for the Sun

"One day this is going to be over- can you imagine that day? How we'll come out into the sun and laugh and hug and sing and dance and hold hands? I'm living for that day. It'll be like nothing we've experienced before."
– Glennon Doyle, author of *Untammed Warrior*, March 2020

When we got home, the house felt so still compared to all of the noise and staff bustling around at the hospital. We spent much of our time on the couch holding Lucy: that seemed to be what she liked the most. Taking turns watching her, we alternated who got to nap - we were instantly exhausted from the sleep deprivation.

The postpartum pain was intense. Even if I merely shifted my weight while sitting on the couch, it caused me to tense up. I knew that billions of women had done this before me, especially under dire conditions, but it just excruciating. I had to laugh when the doctors discussed "pain management" and sent me home with Tylenol and Motrin. That's it? After a grade 3 tear, over-the-counter medication seemed insufficient. Slowly, every few days, certain pains began to subside. Suddenly, I could get into bed without help, then I could sit down without wincing, finally I no longer needed to sit on an ice pack. Even though those physical pains started to subside, my anxiety kicked in, most often at night.

I'd wake up in the middle of the night in a panic, afraid that I had somehow fallen asleep while nursing and suffocated Lucy between the covers. Every time, she was safely in her bassinet. This heart-pounding panic happened nightly for weeks on end, and then a surge of adrenaline gave way to exhaustion as

I nursed her in the middle of the night. One time I was so exhausted nursing Lucy at 3 a.m. that I slapped my cheeks to wake up.

I struggled to get the hang of breastfeeding, finding it difficult to tell if Lucy was getting enough milk. At Pat's encouragement, I did a tele-session with Tina, a lactation consultant. It felt awkward to show Tina what I was doing, as she peered through the computer, trying to assess whether or not Lucy was successfully latching on. The more she talked and asked questions about how things were going, the more I could feel a lump in my throat. A single tear spilled down my cheek, as more tears quickly gathered. When Tina asked if I was okay, Pat looked at me: surprised and sad to see me crying while holding Lucy. Through the computer screen, the consultant said, "I know you're working really hard to take care of Lucy, but you also need to take care of yourself. It can be really hard for mothers to try to step away, especially right now with Covid. Even if you just go for a walk for 30 minutes a few days a week, it'll give you some separation. And that's good for all of you: mom, dad, and baby."

After we finished the consultation, I couldn't stop crying. It was the first major cry since Lucy was born, and it was as if every emotion just flowed out of me. Snot ran down my cheeks as my whole face became blotchy with red crying spots. Pat, who had been right by my side anytime I needed anything, said, "Please let me help you. I love you so much and you need to take care of yourself. I know I can't feed Lucy, but I can hold her, read to her, and change her. I know you want to do it all, and you don't like to accept help, but you need to take time for yourself. I am Lucy's dad and want to take care of her too."

An hour later, I took our dog Heshie out for a short walk for some "me time." Even though the first couple of walks around the block felt exhausting, the walks gave Pat the opportunity for one-on-one time with Lucy and for me to clear my head.

At three weeks postpartum, I finally felt like I could move more comfortably. I was missing running. It was one of the longest stretches I'd ever gone without running in over a decade. I cautiously put on my running clothes - I thought I'd just test things out to see how my body felt. I cautiously stepped outside in the cool evening air (a welcome change from the humidity of June). I hesitated to pick up the pace - my body felt so different without my pregnant belly. Even though it was slow and I felt like I was goose-stepping to adjust to my postpartum body, I began to relax. It was if someone released the pressure valve that had been building up.

Admittedly, I went back to running too early (the recommendation is to wait after your six-week checkup). My hips ached, even from just running three miles a couple of times a week. Despite the pain, I couldn't hold off from running any longer - I knew that this would help me cope with postpartum anxiety. Running shut my brain off from worries I had about my daughter or concerns about the pandemic. Running offered a sense of normalcy to a world that seemed so radically different from just a few months before.

The weekend of my birthday (June 19th), my parents came to D.C. to meet Lucy. At my request, they waited three weeks, so that I had a chance to get settled into breastfeeding, sleep deprivation, and what it's like caring for a newborn. It was a wonderful weekend and gave me a chance to take a breath, knowing that extra hands were around. They instantly melted upon holding her for the first time. The anticipation of holding their first (and likely only) grandchild was immense to begin with, but combining that with the pandemic only accentuated their desire to meet Lucy. When she slept, I peppered my parents with questions: what I was like as a newborn, favorite things they liked to do with us as babies, and what to expect in these next few months. My parents have always been invaluable resources, but I felt a new level of that support with Lucy. As I waved goodbye with Lucy in my arms, I was sad to see them go, especially because Pat was headed back to work the next day for the first time since Lucy was born.

That night, as he rocked Lucy to sleep, Pat sang "Remember me" from the Disney movie *Coco*, which brought me to tears:

Know that I'm with you
The only way that I can be
Until you're in my arms again
Remember me

He held her so tightly, and she looked at him while he sang, utterly transfixed. Although Pat hadn't been around a lot of babies before Lucy, he fell into fatherhood so naturally. His ability to soothe her in the middle of the night was remarkable. Through patient and loving rocking, Pat could get our daughter to at last fall back asleep.

When Pat left for work that Monday morning, he said solemnly, "Please take advantage of this time with her," knowing I had six more weeks of maternity leave remaining. I nodded, trying to swallow the lump in my throat.

When Pat shut the door, the house fell deafeningly silent. "It's just us now," I whispered to Lucy, who was asleep in my arms. What the heck were we going to do now?

***

With time, maternity leave settled into a routine. Each morning, I walked with Lucy before it got too hot out. Those walks felt post-apocalyptic as we passed everyone wearing masks. Lucy had no idea that the world was or could be any different. Typically, within a few minutes of pushing her in the stroller, she'd drift off to sleep. However, when she was almost two months old, Lucy's eyes suddenly widened in the stroller, as if she became realized there was a whole larger world around her. From that point on, Lucy fought falling asleep as long as possible. She was so eager to glimpse every tree, flower, and person in sight. Those small moments, as she slipped into the next stage of discovery, were what I enjoyed most.

My parenting books were not written for raising an infant during a pandemic. The advice of "get out of the house, take your child places, socialize with friends and family" was terribly non-relevant. We only ever entered another indoor space to go to the hospital for Lucy's wellness visits with her pediatrician, Dr. Grey. Sweating in the D.C. heat, I pushed Lucy's stroller through the hospital halls, as people sought to glimpse Lucy - certainly one of the few happy things for people to see in the hospital. Sitting alone and masked in the waiting room, I felt so vulnerable. Would the pediatrician think I was a bad mom? Was Lucy progressing with her neck strength? Was she gaining enough weight?

Each visit, Dr. Grey happily greeted us. As she engaged with Lucy, I could feel myself relaxing. She never offered criticism - just encouragement and suggestions. My eyes often welled up in relief. In her moments of compassion, Dr. Grey reminded me a lot of my best friend Kathleen, also a physician. The similarity offered a comfort - something I desperately needed.

***

So much of being a new parent became wrapped up in the isolation of the pandemic. I had anticipated that being a new mom would feel lonely, but the mandatory confinement of quarantining was painful. I FaceTimed with my parents every day: they could see their granddaughter and I could have some adult interaction while Pat was at work.

I had too much time on my own to think and wonder about what life would be like without the pandemic. I had imagined that during maternity leave, I'd take Lucy to the library for storytime or to a petting zoo to see the animals. Reading Lucy a book about zoo animals brought tears to my eyes: I felt like all of the dreams I had for her first year were lost to the pandemic. I had to remind myself that those early experiences were more for me as a parent, and that Lucy would have no memory of them (nor miss their absence). Moreover, Lucy was such a happy baby and delighted in being read to, looking out the window, and laughing at our dog. Her ability to find joy in the little things gave me optimism for our larger (and often scarier) world.

In the first few months of Lucy's life, I witnessed both the best and worst in people. Even though they couldn't provide us with in-person support when Lucy was born, our friends and family sent food, baby supplies, clothes: anything to keep us afloat. Then there were others who acted like it was an enormous burden to wear a piece of cloth to protect themselves and others. When my sole responsibility was to protect this fragile newborn, it angered me to see so many people acting recklessly in the face of the virus. If, when I was out on a walk with Lucy and saw an unmasked group of people, I tried steer the stroller in a different direction. Even though the likelihood of a short encounter like that was unlikely going to give me or Lucy Covid, I didn't want to risk it.

One evening, I was walking with Lucy, and an unmasked man came up beside our stroller. "Cute baby," he remarked, as I tried to push the stroller faster. I muttered a quick "thanks," and then to my alarm, he bent over to peek into the stroller, his uncovered face hovering too close to my baby girl. "You're not wearing a mask, please give us some space," I asked, the urgency rising in my voice. He stormed off, yelling "I don't fucking care about a mask!" Rationally, I knew that the brief encounter was not going to lead to us contracting Covid, but I was furious. And I was worn out: parenting a newborn during the pandemic was exhausting.

Kathleen, who had provided sisterly guidance and support my entire adult life, called regularly to check in. A mom herself to two young girls, her memories of new motherhood remained vivid. During one of our conversations, Kathleen asked how Lucy was sleeping. I couldn't get any words out. I kept swallowing the lumps in my throat. I felt so lonely and vulnerable. The space between us on the phone felt both non-existent and enormous. "It's so hard, Kathleen," I cried. "She doesn't sleep. I love her so much, but I'm so tired."

She always knew the right thing to say: "This is really hard, Vanessa. It is incredibly exhausting to be a parent. You are doing a great job. And you are doing this during a freaking pandemic. Even though Pat is there, the two of you are mainly doing this on your own - it's not meant to be like that. You're a great mom to Lucy - you know that, right?" I nodded, even though she couldn't see me. As they had been for over twenty years, those phone calls were a lifeline when I needed it the most. With each call, I got a bit of a lift. I wasn't the only one who was burned out because of the pandemic, and that things would improve as Lucy got older, especially with the promise of the vaccine. I clung to that hope. Even so, it often wasn't enough to assuage my fears that I wasn't taking the best care of my baby.

When she was about two months old, Lucy's sleep began to lengthen. Being able to sleep for more than two or three hours in a row was amazing. A few weeks later, she began to sleep for eight hours consecutively. We felt like we broke through the cycle of sleeplessness and could breathe again. I could put Lucy down at 10 p.m., have her wake up between 5-6 a.m., nurse her back to sleep, and then have a few hours to myself before Pat went to work. This was perfect timing, as I was getting ready to go back to work myself.

Even though I knew that going back to work remotely was going to present its challenges, I was also eager to return to work to break up the monotony. There was little to no variation in my day, and while I enjoyed all of the time with Lucy, I needed at least some semblance of engagement with people on a regular basis, even if it was only over Zoom.

**

I went back to work when Lucy was ten weeks old. Those first few months, she wasn't very mobile and was often just happy to be held on my lap. Sitting on the couch, I Zoomed with students, offering guidance on how to plan their fall schedules, sign up for internships, and other academic advice. As long as I nursed her beforehand (I was also grateful that I had the ability to turn off my laptop camera if I needed to nurse on demand), Lucy contently sat through my meetings. Work kept me busy and the weeks started to go by quickly.

When she turned five months old, I started to run with Lucy in the stroller. Even though my heart pounded from pushing the extra weight up the hills in our neighborhood, the runs were so fun. As the world whizzed by her, I felt at peace because I knew she was safe, getting fresh air, and enjoying herself. A few days a week, Pat came home from work early enough so I could run before sunset, but being able to take Lucy out on my own time provided a new sense of flexibility and freedom, instead of waiting around for Pat to relieve me. Wrapped in a fleece blanket that kept Lucy warm all winter, I was able to run almost every day. Those runs were the happiest, easiest hour of parenting each day. They provided me with something to look forward to, which was so important as our contact with the outside world remained limited.

Thankfully, my parents came for monthly visits in the fall. I was grateful that they were willing to limit their socialization with others so that we could know that their visits were safe. They carefully planned their seven-hour car trips: strategizing how to limit their stops and reduce exposure. Each visit, it felt as if the final day was filled with a bit of desperation, emotion. Hugs were a lot longer, because we weren't sure when we'd see each other again. I monitored the D.C. Covid case count daily, which also listed the ages of any residents who died. Seeing the numbers of people who died from it in their 50s and 60s had me concerned - was this visit going to kill my parents? I desperately wanted them to be an important part of Lucy's life, but also worried that it was selfish to have them visit. It was a lot to worry about, and though I had a lot more stability and support than many during the pandemic, my anxiety was picking up again.

One thing that was challenging about working from home with Lucy was all of the alone time in my head. I was always grateful when I had Zoom meetings scheduled, as it gave me an opportunity to feel connected with others. But in the moments when I was sitting on the floor with Lucy, playing with her, it was easy for my worries about work, Lucy, and the pandemic to run rampant again, especially once she stopped sleeping through the night.

Not only did Lucy stop sleeping through the night in November, she was waking up every few hours like when she was a newborn. *How were we back to this?* I had read about the different sleep regressions that babies often experience. This one never seemed to end. Those middle of the night crying jags were one of the worst parts of parenting a baby. Lucy cried inconsolably: her face turned red, and no matter what we tried, Pat and I couldn't calm her down. Seeing our child in distress without any sense of what was causing her such misery was painful. I cried too - I couldn't bear to see her like that. Pat would jump in, able to put up emotional guardrails when I couldn't. When she finally fell asleep, I continued to sob - I hated feeling helpless and unable to soothe her.

I felt worse than I did when she was first born, because now she was active during the day and not sleeping well during the night. It was one thing to be up at 4 a.m. and not have to work the next day. It was another to be waking up every few hours, knowing that work awaited me too. Pat was suffering too. This was miserable.

We then tried to do sleep training, where we didn't pick up Lucy and just rubbed her back while she cried in the crib. Our little baby looked at us, distraught while we rubbed her back to try to soothe her for hours. In the beginning, I tried to be optimistic at the start each night: maybe *this* was the night that she would sleep longer. When it was time to put Lucy in the crib, I silently uttered a "Hail Mary" prayer, hoping that the Virgin Mary's intercession could induce a night of peaceful sleep. Again and again, Lucy only cried. Even if it wasn't my turn to be the one to soothe her, it was impossible to drown out the noise. Her crying wrenched my heart open. I could not provide comfort to my own child and I felt like a terrible mom.

Not only were the nights difficult, but there were times when Lucy only napped for ten to twenty minutes in the crib before waking up crying. This brought me to tears too - every time she woke up, she was crying: a plaintive wail that rang through the house, like a fire engine siren, again and again until she was picked up.

Part of what was hard was that Lucy was such a happy

baby when she was awake. She spent her wake periods giggling and smiling all of the time. How could this be the same baby?

Pat and I were stumbling through work exhausted and miserable. Three weeks into sleep training, at 6 a.m., I started to bring her in the bed with me. I couldn't see trying to soothe her back asleep again. Cradling her in one arm, I'd grab my laptop from my nightstand and start working on emails. After a few mornings of quiet, combined with nights where we were lucky to string together a couple of hours of sleep, I started to wonder if she should sleep in our bed.

I called Kathleen for advice, as I remembered that she co-slept with both of her daughters years before. "Vanessa, I know there are risks, but there are also risks to you not sleeping. I have no regrets about it. I was at a breaking point and once we did, she was sleeping better. I was relieved. You will be too." After Pat and I had a lengthy conversation about it, ultimately deciding that the upsides (our sanity) outweighed the risks, we started bed-sharing with Lucy. She'd always start off in the crib, but once she woke up, she went to bed with us.

If you had told me even two months prior that we'd be bed-sharing, I wouldn't have believed it. I was always adamant we'd never do it - too many risks! I had never publicly shamed anyone for doing it, but I know I silently judged them. But the sleepless nights made me feel like I was losing my mind. I had never switched so fast from one side of a parenting debate to the other.

Lucy did not magically start to sleep through the night. Still, her wakeup periods grew fewer and shorter. I could nurse her for a few minutes, and then we'd all drift back to sleep. The tension started to dissipate. Bedtime was no longer dreaded, and I felt more relaxed. I knew it was a temporary fix to a larger issue. It gave us a chance to breathe and enjoy our time with Lucy: both day and night. We all became happier. Even though it was a pandemic, even though the world felt upside down, the fact that we all slept a little better gave us the opportunity to enjoy the day-to-day moments of raising our baby.

I was surprised that even the pediatrician supported our decision. When Dr. Grey asked at Lucy's nine-month check-up, "has sleep improved at all," knowing that we had been going through a rough patch, I nervously responded, "yes, but that's because we've been bringing her in the bed. We've been taking as many precautions as possible," I said hastily. "Vanessa, you have to pick your battles. You can try again in a few months, but you all need sleep." I breathed a sigh of relief. We were sleeping better and thus more able to enjoy all of the wonderful moments with Lucy during the day, instead of feeling exhausted and resentful. We were turning a corner.

***

As things started to improve with Lucy, it felt like the larger world was turning a corner. After the horrifying insurrection on the Capitol, we collectively exhaled when President Biden was safely inaugurated, bringing about an end to the nightmare of the Trump administration. As an essential member of the State Department, Pat got vaccinated early, which was a relief since he was in the office every day. My parents also got vaccinated early: they could come visit without worry. When I got my first shot in April, tears of joy streamed down my face. Because I was still breastfeeding Lucy, she was also going to get some of the antibodies for the vaccine. I was grateful I could give her this protection.

I knew things were improving as my journal entries to Lucy were becoming more joyful.

***

April 7, 2021

Today was as close as we could get to a perfect day. You spent the first part of the morning playing in the doorframe, happily watching all of the cars driving by and people waving to you from the sidewalk. You then took a record 2.5-hour nap. Even though I could see on the baby monitor that you stirred a few times, you kept comforting yourself and going back to sleep. I was able to do a lot of writing, and then when you woke up, we had a nice lunch together. We sat outside on a blanket, and you watched all of the planes go by, craning your neck to see everything. It's adorable when you clap as they fly overhead. You somehow managed to take another 1.5-hour nap (maybe you're having a growth spurt?), and then we went for a run on my favorite trail. You were so happy, babbling the whole time, and sometimes literally laughing out loud.

Once your dad came home, we were able to have a family dinner together. Your dad then went on a run, while you happily played in the playpen, and I was able to clean up. After your bath, your dad read you a story and you quickly went to bed, which gave your dad and I some time to spend together. It was a practically perfect day.

There are times when the day doesn't go to plan. Not great naps, or I have a frustrating day at work, or your dad has to work late. None of that happened today. It wasn't a magical day filled with super exciting things - just simple and happy. I love you, sweet girl.

Epilogue: The First Birthday

So many people told us that a baby's first birthday is really more of a celebration for the parents. There was such a sense of relief and accomplishment in making it through the first year. Lucy was born during the height of the first wave of the pandemic. By the time of her first birthday on May 26, 2021, both Pat and I were fully vaccinated and no new variants were in sight that summer. I was so frightened of everything when Lucy was born: she was so small and helpless, and adding into new parent anxiety was pandemic anxiety. Although we couldn't completely relax, getting vaccinated made it feel like we could be a little less afraid of the world. We started to eat at outdoor restaurants, take Lucy to the playground, and meet up with other vaccinated people – all things I had been looking forward to for so long.

Turning the corner allowed me to soak up all of this time with Lucy and get to watch the beautiful personality of our child develop. Having spent nearly every waking hour with her, I loved watching how she observes the world. One of my favorite things about Lucy as a baby was that she already loved to read. I put a few books on the floor each morning, and she thumbed through the pages, carefully studying the colorful pictures. It brought me endless delight to watch her become engrossed with books, as I did as a child and still do now.

As my parents have corroborated, Lucy is already more adventurous than I ever was. She loves to run around in the grass at the park and climb *up* the slide at the playground. When Lucy senses an opportunity to scurry away and get into mischief, she seizes the opportunity. She runs without any hesitation, and I hope that boldness and curiosity stay with her as she grows up.

There are so many things I want to teach Lucy: how to read, how to swim (hopefully, she'll take to it faster than me), how to ride a bike (again, hopefully faster than me - I was slow when it came to anything that required coordination), but I hope she'll be able to learn from me and my anxiety as she starts to navigate through the world. I didn't know how to navigate or describe my emotions when problems seemed insurmountable. I internalized so much when, had I shared these concerns with my family, professors, or a therapist earlier on, I could've better learned how to cope with those feelings. I didn't have to go through life with a constant knot in my stomach or inability to sleep.

I want Lucy to know that her feelings are real and valid, and that she's not the only one to feel like that. I had always been aware of the millions of people who suffered from anxiety and depression - I had assured myself that my problems weren't "that bad" comparison to what others were dealing with.

Although I will never be fully rid of my anxiety, I have learned that I can manage it and live with it. Even in moments when it feels relentless, it can pass. Just like there is a sense of peace and calm when I watch Lucy's little chest rise and fall as she breathes in her deep sleep, I can breathe in peace and exhale anxiety.

It is marvelous to watch Lucy's ceaseless determination to joyfully discover the world. Having her in our lives provides more motivation to keep going. Not just because she needs me, but because I want to be alive for her and our family. I don't want to miss anything in her life. I want to see her go to school, make friends, have a family - anything and everything she sets her mind to do.

Lucy is the purest expression of joy that I know. She squeals in excitement over the smallest things: being handed a new toy or even a box of pasta to play with. She loves our dog and she bursts into giggles anytime Heshie walks by. I want to see all of those moments.

I know that for sure because there are so times that I've

spent with Lucy when I've thought to myself, "I would've missed this."

Of course, when I was in my dark place, there was no futuristic voice that could shout, "One day you'll have an amazing daughter. You need to stick around long enough for her to exist! There are so many great moments to come, both big and small, that will not come into fruition if you are no longer a part of this world." I kept so much of myself locked up for no one else to find out for what - to preserve the idea that I was holding it together. That approach came at a cost. I saw failure as an identity, when it's really just a moment. I needed to hang on, even though the darkness and sadness felt crushing. I couldn't see at that moment that life can be more magnificent than these moments of doubt, despair, and failure.

I think part of the reason it's upsetting to think about is that I worry that one day, my very joyful baby could entertain those same thoughts. After all, her own mother has struggled with this. I look at all of her pure expressions of happiness and am terrified of what could happen.

To my most beautiful daughter, if you ever feel even a little like this, please keep going. There is a way out and I will be with you on the other side. And if I had ever told my own mom this, she would've said the same thing. "Keep going." "We love you. "There is more than this one sad moment, and so many beautiful things are still to come."

It's the lesson I keep relearning and will teach Lucy as well: it's a marathon, not a sprint, and there are countless people to cheer us on and catch us when we fall.

What Did You Think of It's a Marathon, Not a Sprint?

Thank you for purchasing *It's a Marathon, Not a Sprint*! I know you could have picked any number of books to read, but you picked this book and for that I am extremely grateful.

I hope that it added value and quality to your everyday life. If so, it would be really nice if you could share this book with your friends and family by posting it on social media. You can tag me @VRCinDC.

If you enjoyed this book and found some benefit in reading this, I'd like to hear from you and hope that you could take some time to post a review on Amazon and/or Goodreads. Your feedback and support will help me to greatly improve my writing craft for future projects and make this book even better.

I wish you all the best!

-Vanessa

Acknowledgements

I am filled with gratitude to all of those who stood at the mile markers and aid stations along the way to the finish line of this book.

Thank you to Mark Remy and Rachel Toor, who spoke to me about the publishing process. Thanks to Leonard Cassuto, Alexi Pappas, and David Perry, who wrote early blurbs for the book, and special thanks to Elizabeth Clor for writing the forward for the book.

To Kathrine Switzer, thank you for your constant support and inspiring so many of us women to become fearless.

Thank you to all of my running groups: Pacers Running, the MCM Forum, and the Loop. Thank you to Sarah Spalding for being an amazing coach.

Since I was a child, my teachers at Spencerport Central Schools supported and encouraged my academic interests, especially my love of reading. My professors at Holy Cross and The Catholic University of America played an indelible role in my academic career, especially Lorraine Attreed, Jennifer Davis, Kate Jansen, Jennifer Paxton, and Caroline Sherman.

For those who generously read and offered feedback on early drafts of the book: Jennifer Davis, Tom and Nicole Gordon, Erika Howder, Karen McCormick, Micalena Sallavanti, and Aia Yousef.

I am grateful for the warmth and hospitality that has come from my colleagues in the College Dean's Office at Georgetown University: Marlene Canlas, Jessica Ciani-Dausch, Thom Chiarolanzio, Bernie Cook, Erin Force, Tad Howard, Javier Jiménez Westerman, Sarah Lim, Sue Lorenson, Mike Parker, Kathryn Wade, Keshia Woods, Aia Yousef, and Stefan Zimmers.

My students at Georgetown University have provided me with a renewed sense of purpose in sharing my story about confronting my own anxieties about academia.

My grad school roommate Julie Yarwood has a razor-sharp memory and often helped fill in the gaps of conversations I had forgotten over the years.

My "Ride or Die" friends Micalena Sallavanti and Kate Miedrich have continued to offer me support even though we all live in different states.

Writing this book brought back many memories of my friends at Holy Cross, Catholic University, and the Center for Talented Youth. I'm so grateful for your friendship.

Nearly eight years after they stood on the altar next to me on my wedding day, my bridesmaids continue to play a fundamental role in my life: Amanda Daxon, Sara Tully, and Jennifer Olsen. Kathleen Mannava remains the closest person I'll ever have to a sister, and I can't imagine my life without you.

Thank you to my in-laws, the Corcorans, for continuing to make me feel like a welcome member of the family.

I'm fortunate to have such a supportive extended family, both on the Taylor and McGuire sides of the family. I don't take it for granted that my grandparents, Bob and Lucille McGuire, have witnessed so many of my major milestones. Naming Lucy after you was such a thrill, Grandma.

My sibling Nova was instrumental in the editing process and offered many great ideas and feedback. I appreciate all that you've done for me.

The two people least surprised that I ever decided to write a book are my parents, Doug and Judy Taylor, who nurtured my reading and writing habits from an early age. They instilled confidence in me, and offered reassurance when doubts threatened to cloud my progress. I'm grateful for their unending support.

My husband Pat rode the roller coaster of emotions with me through the dissertation process, and came out of the other side. Having you here to cheer me on during this new writing process was all the more fun (and way fewer tears this time). I'm glad we get to raise our wonderful child together.

And for my beautiful daughter, Lucy. The joy you have brought to our lives has surpassed our wildest dreams. Thank you for being the brightest (and silliest) light and giving me a renewed sense of purpose to keep going.

About The Author

Vanessa R. Corcoran

Although she spent her childhood with her nose in a book, ducking when any ball was thrown in her direction, Vanessa is now a 2-time Boston Marathon finisher, and has run over 100 road races. Currently an advising dean and adjunct professor of history at Georgetown University, Vanessa earned her Ph.D. in medieval history from  The Catholic University of America. Vanessa lives in Washington D.C. with her husband Patrick and their daughter, Lucy. This is her first book.

Praise For Author

"Self-proclaimed no-talent Vanessa Corcoran has scored the Triple: A PhD, a book and a Boston-qualifying marathon. In It's A Marathon, Not a Sprint, she writes with a racer's power, a runner's lyrical rhythm, and an achiever's honesty and wisdom to galvanize us, and show how we, too, can persist, and overcome the impossible."

- KATHRINE SWITZER, FIRST WOMAN TO OFFICIALLY REGISTER AND RUN THE BOSTON MARATHON; AUTHOR, MARATHON WOMAN; AND CO-FOUNDER, 261 FEARLESS NON-PROFIT

"As a story of writing and running toward a goal, Vanessa Corcoran's "It's a Marathon, Not a Sprint" is a courageous testimonial to the value of true grit. It's also a thoroughly entertaining read."

Leonard Cassuto, author of The New PhD: How to Build a Better Graduate Education

- LEONARD CASSUTO, AUTHOR OF THE NEW PHD: HOW TO BUILD A BETTER GRADUATE EDUCATION

"A beautiful memoir of the author's intertwined challenges of running farther and faster, while also pursuing the deepest study possible of the medieval past. Both journeys required her to not only train her body and mind, but to come to know herself on a deeper level than she might have imagined possible. I spent the book cheering the author forward at every turn, hoping she wouldn't stumble, and confident she'd get back up again when she did."

- DAVID PERRY, AUTHOR OF THE BRIGHT AGES

"Vanessa's story is exactly what we need more of in the world today: it's a personal, honest, and brave account of struggling with - and overcoming - depression, and will surely inspire others to embrace their own mental health growth."

- ALEXI PAPPAS, OLYMPIAN AND AUTHOR OF BRAVEY: CHASING DREAMS, BEFRIENDING PAIN, AND OTHER BIG IDEAS

Made in the USA
Monee, IL
16 March 2022